REVOLUTIONARY BIBLE STUDY

REVOLUTIONARY BIBLE STUDY

SeedSowers Publishing
Jacksonville, Florida

Revolutionary Bible Study

Printed in the United States of America

In Memorium

He had just been asked by Billy Graham to be in charge of follow-up of converts in the Billy Graham campaign. He arrived in Fort Worth, Texas one month after the campaign ended. (At that time I was an eighteen-year old seminary student.)

He was in the city for one week. Somehow, I ended up being his chauffeur! He was a unique, dynamic man. He made a great impact on me as a new Christian. (He gave me my "B-ration," set on small cards with Bible verses on them.)

He died shortly thereafter in a boating accident. He was a major influence on thousands of Christians in their relationship to Scripture, and a cherished friend.

Daws Trotman
Founder of The Navigators

MUCH MORE THAN A BOOK

Revolutionary Bible Study is a monumental, even historic, breakthrough in the Christian endeavor. For the first time in centuries, we have a totally new way to study the New Testament. This unprecedented breakthrough gives us a clarity in understanding the New Testament that never before has been known. This book also liberates the Scripture and the reader from the hindrance of tradition which has been blocking our understanding for 1800 years. Had this book been written in the year 300, every century would have had a model of the first century to deal with. At the very least, they would have known many renewals troughout the ages. This is because *Revolutionary Bible Study* gives us a clear view of what the first Christian century was truly like.

The result of 1800 years of the chaotic arrangement of the books of the New Testament ends here. This book brings forth the clearest view of the original practice of our faith in an ever-moving, forward manner.

Revolutionary Bible Study may not only revolutionize the way we study the Bible, but it has the potential to revolutionize our lives.

How unique is this book?

Imagine two libraries. One library has all the books ever written on the New Testament in the order in which they are arranged in your Bible. The second library? It contains only one book...*this* book.

It took a student of theology a lifetime of studying early Roman history and an archaeology aficionado who has spent forty years reading the New Testament in the order it was written, in order to give us this book.

WELCOME TO A NEW WORLD OF BIBLE STUDY!

This book has no chapters! The years between A.D. 30 and 70 *are* the chapters.

Use the Tables of Contents to Find:

TABLE OF CONTENTS – I

Locating the Chapters in Acts by
This Book's Page Numbers

TABLE OF CONTENTS – II

What Happened, by Year
30–70

TABLE OF CONTENTS – II
(*CONTINUED*)

What Happened, by Year
30–70

TABLE OF CONTENTS – III

Background to Paul's Thirteen Letters

UNIQUE WAYS TO USE THIS BOOK

- Read any *chapter* in Acts and learn from this book what happened in that chapter. Did any letter of the New Testament get written that year? Did anything happen in Israel which influenced the events found in that chapter? Did anything in that chapter in Acts refer to something that happened in the Roman Empire? Did that historical event influence what was recorded in the chapter?
- Look at any *year* between 30 and 70 and find what happened that year in the empire, in Israel, among Christians; and find out if any letter of the New Testament was written that year . . . and see it in its setting and surrounding events.

THE ULTIMATE SACRED COW

In my second year in the seminary, I lived in Rome. I had earlier lived in the Holy Lands. While tracing the footsteps of Paul, I noticed that the times and places Paul wrote his letters did not follow the order as found in my New Testament. This bothered me. Why are we not reading Paul in the order he wrote his letters? Would this not give us much more clarity? Then came a remark made by one of my teachers which caused me to realize that chronological order was of no interest to Bible teachers: "All the T letters of Paul are together in one place. Wasn't that nice of God to put all the *T's* together?"

My startled reaction: Paul wrote I Thessalonians in the year *51*. Paul wrote I Timothy in the year *67*. Yes, the *T* epistles are bunched together, yet *seventeen years* apart. This is no way to understand the New Testament.

So it began. May it now also begin for you.

Turn to the table of contents of your New Testament. The years in which Paul wrote his thirteen letters bear no similarity to the order in which those letters appear.

How came to be this mess?

This odd arrangement came about in a bookbinder's shop in about A.D. 200. Writings were arranged by *length*. Paul's letters, therefore, are arranged in your New Testament by his longest letter down to his shortest letter. In 1800 years we seem not to have cared about their proper order.

It was after departing the Holy Lands that I moved to Rome. It was there I first began drawing together the material found in this book. That was the beginning. That was over forty years ago and a mountain of research and writing.

The seminary had given me very little first-century history. Christian books on the subject were grossly inadequate. (And Paul's letters... they remained un-rearranged!) The word *context* was employed, but meagerly. First-century Christian history should be chronological and tri-level... Rome, Israel, Christian... and forward moving. The historic order must be organic, not dictated by a bookbinder who died over 1700 years ago. This failure leaves us with great gaps in our understanding of the Word of God.

Those whom we depend upon for scholarship have neglected the blending together of the empire's history, Israel's history, and the Christian part of the first-century story. Only then do we have the entire context and history in the order it happened.

In Rome, I was given excellent exposure to not only the traditional first-century history of the empire, but also something which was just beginning. It is now called church archaeology. Despite the fact that I was a dyed-in-the-wool Protestant, and even more, a Baptist, I owe a great deal to Jesuit scholars who put up with a nineteen-year-old kid challenging just about everything they taught, especially their interpretation of church archaeology.* I was allowed access to places and material to which Protestants today do not have access.

---

* Almost all biblical archaeology centered on the Old Testament. Church archaeology centers on archaeological evidence found after the year 30 to the year 100. Even now, this is an emerging discipline neglected in today's seminary education.

It became a passion to know exactly what happened from 4 B.C. through A.D. 70...and especially encompassing Acts and Paul's letters.

This book is a forty-plus-year result of that passion.

The church, from Pentecost to the destruction of Jerusalem, is where we should return. There we rediscover what emperors, priests, soldiers, believers, *et al.*, did. In so doing, for the first time, we get a good look at those years *and* what the church really is. These discoveries can be made only if we embrace Acts and Paul's letters, not in the jumbled order in which they were passed down to us, but in the light of all the surrounding events.

As simple as this is, it is earthshaking, cataclysmic, and revolutionary. It can also make a mess of your comfortable Scriptural understanding. That is the intent of this book.

What you will learn is that what we do today has nothing to do with what Christians did in Century One.

So vast, so different, and so very, very biblical, these discoveries create a challenge to all of us.

> There is no similarity to how we practice present-day evangelical Christianity as over against the way the church practiced Christianity in Century One.

WHAT TO EXPECT

Placing Paul's letters in their proper order and then bringing together all the surrounding context opens a whole new world to us.

Now, after four decades of living in this ever forward-flowing way of knowing the Scripture, I invite you into a unique, panoramic landscape of a journey through Century One, year by year, and the writings of the New Testament, book by book. It is my prayer, my dream, that God's Word will become utterly new to you ... from one-dimensional to three-dimensional, perhaps making reading the Word of God sheer joy.

Now, may your journey never end as you find an organic view of the New Testament. May this book mark the beginning of a new day, a new era, a restoration in biblical understanding.

Gene Edwards
Roanoke, Alabama

No One Has Understood the New Testament For 1800 Years

The New Testament is so chaotically arranged that it would be hard to image that anyone—you, I or the world's greatest scholar—could ever get a clear understanding of what the New Testament is saying. Such is the disastrous result of this present arrangement of the New Testament letters . . . a chaotic arrangement with which we have been living for 1800 years.

Just how bad is this chaos? Read Paul's letters: these letters are arranged in a jumble, without context, sequence or setting. Take for example Romans, which is Paul's sixth letter but listed first. Romans was written in the year 58; then you turn the page and there before you are I and II Corinthians. Both letters were written before Romans . . . in 57. Next you turn to Galatians. You are now reading backwards. Why? Galatians was written in the year 50, *seven* years *before* Corinthians and *eight* years *before* Romans. Next come Ephesians, Philippians and Colossians, which were written in the year 63. I Timothy and Titus were written in 65, with II Timothy written in 67. (Hold on to your hat.) Suddenly you come to I and II Thessalonians which were written way back in the year 51 and 52, which is *sixteen* years *before* II Timothy. Finally, you turn to the little letter Philemon—you will now jump from the year 52 all the way to year 63.

No human mind could come up with a clear context, setting or sequence after passing through this jumbled maze.

Now look at Paul's letters in the order in which he wrote them. Automatically, there emerges the *first-century story*. Suddenly you have a *new* New Testament . . . one you clearly understand.

HERE'S HOW TO DO THIS

Letter	Year Written
Galatians, I & II Thessalonians	50, 51 & 52
I & II Corinthians	57
Romans	58
Ephesians, Colossians, Philemon &	
Philippians	63
I Timothy & Titus	65
II Timothy	67

In this book you find that clear sequence plus added context and setting, so you can finally understand the New Testament.

Such is the purpose of this book.

No matter how much you exhort them, most Christians will not long continue to read their New Testament. There is a reason.

Most Christians who read the New Testament never read it again. Those who keep reading it cannot understand what it says.

When you have finished this book, all of that will change. Let's see!

A Drunk Has Much to Teach Us

A drunk staggers into his hotel room. He is desperate to change his life. He reaches for the Bible and opens it to the first page of the New Testament. He is greeted with two pages of genealogy! Is that understandable? No! Yet, this is how the greatest book in history opens...and has opened for over 1,800 years. Furthermore, it seems no one has suggested changing this unbelievable opening. No, the New Testament is not understandable because it is fettered by too many religious traditions.

Let us begin by changing this ridiculous introduction! The New Testament *should* open with the Gospel of Mark. (Mark was written *before* Matthew.) Mark is simple, clear, brief, beautiful, and a perfect introduction to the life of the Lord Jesus Christ.

This order of the first two Gospels is a *small* sacred cow. Now look at the entire New Testament. It cannot be understood, not as it is.

Fifteen Hundred Years of No One's Being Able to Understand the New Testament

For 1500 years, the New Testament was only in Latin, a *dead* language. But to place the New Testament in a language other than Latin carried the death penalty.

Is that unbelievable? While that was a Catholic tradition, now look at the Protestant tradition. For over three hundred years, we Protestants also had the New Testament in a dead language. If anyone suggested that we Protestants read the New Testament in another version, he was looked upon with a jaundiced eye, suspiciously eyed as a possible heretic. This was *Protestant* religious tradition (King James English), and it fettered the Bible for over three hundred years. King James English died in 1670, but it was read *exclusively* for three hundred years after the death of the language.

Hindering religious tradition has chained the New Testament from being understood, almost from the time it was written; and the Word of God is still fettered and chained. We have a far greater tradition to which we have clung for 1800 years that makes it utterly impossible to understand the New Testament. The New Testament still not understandable?

Impossible?

Let's see.

IMPOSSIBLE TO DECODE

Paul's letters are arranged in pure chaos. Even if you are a Greek scholar, you still cannot possibly understand the New Testament. You can quote the entire New Testament? It matters not! You can quote the New Testament in Greek? This will not help; you still cannot understand it.

Why?

It is because of the bizarre way Paul's letters are arranged. Further, we have been using this arrangement for 1800 years. There has been no thought of changing this chaotic order... no thought of untangling this jumble and placing Paul's letters in their proper sequence.

Let it be stated as emphatically as possible: This jumbled way that Paul's letters are arranged prevents all of us from understanding the greatest book ever written. You will never be able to understand what the New Testament is saying until Paul's letters are arranged properly; then everything will change. The tradition-ridden arrangement of Paul's letters must give way, or the New Testament will remain outside of understandability.

It is interesting to observe that Paul's thirteen letters were all very personal. All were full of locations, people, and events. This makes them quite easy to contribute to *The Story*.

Unfortunately, for nearly 1800 years, the theological mind has dominated our faith. Each of Paul's letters has been examined as a stand-alone, with no relationship to the letter that came before or the letter that came after. The humanity of the letters has been ignored. The interwoven connection has been ignored. Surrounding events have been ignored.

The *verse*, not *The Story*, not the interconnection, has reigned as king. As a result, Paul's letters have been given to us as passionless treaties, one-dimensional, static theological treatments. Unwittingly, we have a New Testament that has remained in captivity to the blindness of religious traditions. Bible study has not been Bible study, but a study of verses. All this has left us with virtually no knowledge of *The Story*.

The purpose of this book is to free the New Testament from those 1800 years of old religious tradition and set the Scripture free to be clear and understandable. Place Paul's letters in their correct order, and the New Testament comes alive. Clarity becomes breathtaking.

WHAT IF?

If chronological order had begun in the year 300, there would have never been a Roman Catholic Church, nor a Protestant Church, nor even an evangelical church. Clarity would have prevented it. Instead, by concentrating on *verses* we have been free to invent anything.

If the books of the New Testament had been arranged in the order in which they were written, we would have a model of Century One. We would have seen *The Story* of the first century. As it is, that story is *still* unknown to us. Despite millions of Christian books, we still have no first-century model by which to measure our conjectures that come from verses. Even today, *The Story* cannot be seen.

The power of seeing *The Story* cannot be imagined. See the entire unbroken series of events, and you have unlocked the power of the Word of God.

But what does it mean . . . *The Story*?

STEPS TO UNLOCKING THE NEW TESTAMENT

It is more than just chronology alone.

This book will show you how to discover *The Story*, see the model, and understand the New Testament. Here is a preview of some steps that will help you:

1. Use an excellent translation.
2. Rearrange the New Testament in chronological order.
3. Identify the place, in Acts, where Paul wrote each of his letters. There are six such places.*
4. Take notice that there is a passing of time between each of Paul's letters.
5. Discover what events happened before and after each of those thirteen letters.

[handwritten margin notes: Antioch, Galacia, Ephesus, Corinth, Thessalonica]

   Example: The time between Galatians and I Thessalonians is one-and-one-half years. Fill in those years! When you do, a small part of *The Story* begins to emerge.

   Here is how to fill in the events between letters:

- Acts helps by telling what happened in those one-and-one-half years.
- The events taking place in the Roman Empire can also help.
- Invert each letter; that is, look at the letter not from Paul's view, but from the view of the one receiving the letter. It is called "mirroring."

---

* Acts 15:40; 18:1; 18:5; 19:23; 20:1–3; 20:3–4.

21

• Do this for all thirteen of Paul's letters.

The Story then emerges automatically, all by itself. We see an entire new world of biblical clarity. Never underestimate the power of discovering that story. *The Story* (A.D. 30–70) is every bit as clear as the story in the four Gospels (A.D. 26–30).

THE MODEL

Once you have the books and letters in order, then add dates, times, places, etc. in sequence. Suddenly, you have a model. You have a revolution in Bible study. I hope, dear reader, that can lead to a revolution in your life.

TEARING APART YOUR NEW TESTAMENT!

At one point I will request that you pull apart your New Testament and have it rebound, chronologically. If possible, have a blank page inserted wherever a book of the New Testament begins.

WHAT TRANSLATIONS DO I RECOMMEND?

I can recommend only two translations. One is the *updated* New American Standard (NASV), an excellent New Testament for accuracy. The other is the New Living Translation (NLT), which is excellent for clarity. The NLT has given us what I have considered impossible . . . clarity with accuracy.*

---

* What would it be like for readers to have a New Testament properly arranged? We would have entered a bright, new day. The Word of God would become a fascinating, powerful, captivating, edge-of-your-seat, can't-put-it-down Book. People, even the semi-literate, would be reading such a Book again and again and again!

The years 30–47 are familiar to most Christians. The years 47–70 are unfamiliar to most Christians, even scholars. *Revolutionary Bible Study* begins in the year 30 and ends in the year 70.

Learn these years well, for they are revolutionary!

You and I Are on a Journey through Century One

We will begin our journey with the year 30. When we finish, we will have seen a world, a story, even a New Testament, we have never seen before.

We will blend pertinent parts of the history of the Roman Empire with the history Luke gives to us in the book of Acts. We will see every place, in Acts, where Paul wrote a letter. We will fill in the time which passed between each of Paul's letters, to give you the events and surroundings that influenced the letters and are reflected in the letters. This will reveal to you *The Story* of the years 30–70, enabling you to see the New Testament as a whole and in full dimension.*

MEET THE YEAR 30

The year 30 was one of the most involved in all the Christian faith. The year 30 was the year Jesus Christ was crucified. It was the year of the Day of Pentecost. But it was also a year filled with significant events which affected the Roman Empire, as well as Christians. This blending of two history records allows us to see the Word of God dimensionally, thereby lifting Scripture to a multi-dimensional level and out of our previous one-dimensional, static, flat-surface view of the New Testament. We see the full setting of the events so dear to us.

With that, everything changes. We discover things we have never seen before. A broader world, an unknown world, opens to us.

---

* We have woven some other helps along the way, but have done so unobtrusively.

Example:

The year and circumstances which gave us our very first piece of Christian literature: Galatians was written at Acts 15:40 in the spring of 50. But it was also the year twenty thousand Jews were forced out of Rome, as well as the year of the Jerusalem Council.

That, dear reader, is but one small glimpse of what it means to get a *new* New Testament.

You and I will also see *all* the books in the New Testament, from Galatians to Revelation, in their surrounding circumstances.

You will become accustomed to the feel of what was being talked about in the marketplaces of the empire with every significant event. (The year 51 was just as eventful as the year 50. The marketplace was abuzz with events of that year, too.)

With that, our journey begins.

The
Jerusalem Line
of Churches

The Years 30–47

These are the churches of Judea, Samaria, and Galilee which came out of Jerusalem.

The last church in this line of churches was the Antioch church. The church in Antioch was unique because it began as a Jewish church and became a *Gentile* church.

THERE WILL BE THREE LINES OF CHURCHES:

I.

JERUSALEM
Jewish Churches
One culture

II.

ANTIOCH
Gentile Churches
Different culture in every city
All organic in nature

III.

EPHESIAN
The churches which were raised up by the men Paul trained

The day I first read
the New Testament
in the order it was written . . .
was the best of days.

It may well be one of the best of days for you, too.

BOOK I

THE JERUSALEM LINE 30-47

(The churches which came out of Jerusalem)

Acts 1:1–13:1

- ❧ Jerusalem—Acts Chapters 1–8
- ❧ Jerusalem Churches—Acts Chapters 9–13:1

THE YEAR 30

ACTS 1 AND 2

It is the month of January. The place is Jerusalem.

The year 30 was one of the most remarkable years in all human history. Christ was crucified. The church was born.

But it was also the year the Emperor Tiberius, age 62, moved out of Rome to live a quiet life on the isle of Capri. With him was a deeply troubled eighteen-year-old who would be the next emperor.

The governor of the province of Judea was a man named Pontius Pilate (26–36). In just six years, Pilate would be sent back to Rome in disgrace. He was governor when John the Baptist began his ministry (26), during the crucifixion of Jesus Christ (30), and the Day of Pentecost.

The high priest during those days of John the Baptist, Jesus' ministry, the Day of Pentecost, *and* when Paul was converted was a man named Joseph, son of Caiaphas (18–37).

JERUSALEM

On March 30, Jesus entered Jerusalem. On March 31, a great crowd of people greeted Him with palm branches (Luke 19:29–44).

On April 1 and 2, Jesus taught in the temple. He celebrated the Passover on April 3. He then entered Gethsemane (Luke 22:39–46). Early on the morning of April 4, Jesus was tried, convicted, and then buried at sunset.

On Sunday, April 7, Jesus Christ rose from the dead.

On Sunday, May 29, at about 8:00 in the morning, 120 people were praying in Jerusalem. The Holy Spirit descended as a mighty rushing wind (Acts 2:1–4).

On Monday, May 30, some two thousand or more out-of-town visitors made the decision to remain in Jerusalem. The church was born. The very definition of *ecclesia* began on that day.

How did "church" come into being? Was it a structure created by the apostles? Not at all. *Church life* was spontaneous, part of the divine nature of God expressed in men. The apostles watched and discovered what church was.

Some of the Jewish believers went back home to other parts of the empire. Later, churches would be raised up in some of those provinces.

That same year the beloved teacher, Hillel the Elder, died. Hillel's son, Gamaliel, who had sat at Hillel's feet from his youth, took Hillel's place.

In the province of Cilicia, in the city of Troas, a young man named Saul dreamed of one day coming to Jerusalem to study at the feet of Gamaliel.

It will be twenty more years before the first piece of Christian literature is written.

THE YEAR 31

ACTS 3

ROME AND THE EMPIRE

In Galilee, Antipas, son of Herod the Great, was governor. He had eight years left to live.

Tiberius had formerly ruled the empire from the city of Rome. After that he lived on the beautiful island of Capri, ruling the empire through a deputy named Sejanus. Tiberius heard that Sejanus was going to overthrow Tiberius and seize the throne. Sejanus was tried by the Senate and executed in October of 31.

Such was the talk in the marketplace in every town and city of the empire.

It was also in this year that Tiberius reaffirmed the right of the Jewish people (given by Augustus) to continue to pay their taxes to Jerusalem and to the temple rather than to the Roman Empire.

THE CHURCH

It was in the year 31 that John and Peter entered the temple for prayer. There Peter healed a lame beggar. As a result, hundreds of people believed in Jesus Christ and were added to the church.

Over the next six years (30–35), there were *many* added to the church. Luke tells us that first a *crowd*... then a *multitude*... then *multitudes*... and then *great multitudes*... had become part of the ecclesia in Jerusalem. It has been estimated that there were between seven thousand and twenty thousand believers added to the church during those first six years. This ingathering continued until the year 37, when the growth abruptly ended.

THE YEAR 32

ACTS 4

ROME AND THE EMPIRE

The Day of Pentecost was still in its afterglow when, in the year 32, Pontius Pilate (26–36) provoked a large crowd of Jews by using temple funds for an aqueduct into the city. Pilate put down the resulting outcry with heavy violence.

ISRAEL

Israel lived under the heavy heel of foreign occupiers, yet it was an age of peaceful coexistence with Rome. There was not a single movement trying to overthrow Rome. We will watch that change.

THE CHURCH

Peter was arrested and brought before the council and questioned. Peter, full of the Holy Spirit, declared Jesus Christ before the Jewish leaders.

Peter and John were threatened and then released by the council.

The apostles prayed for courage to continue to speak the Lord's message during persecution.

Upon the healing of a lame man, the Sanhedrin had Peter and John arrested. After an intense encounter with the elders, the two men were released. The citizens of the city praised God for the miracles and signs performed by the apostles (Acts 4).

THE YEAR 33

ACTS 4

ROME AND THE EMPIRE

Two young men were favored to rule the empire upon Tiberius' death. One of them was the great-grandson of Augustus Caesar. His name was Gaius Caligula. In every marketplace in the empire in the year 33, the news was about the marriage of Caligula to a young girl named Claudia, also a descendant of the royal family. Caligula was twenty-one years old. One of his favorite sports was torturing animals. Caligula had a nineteen-year-old sister named Agrippina, who would one day rule Rome for a short time, very short indeed, through her son.

That same year Rome took some of the territory (Judea) that belonged to Israel. This land was given over to the hated Syrians. It was just one more gesture toward the Hebrew people which showed Rome's low opinion of the Jewish nation.

THE CHURCH

The church in Jerusalem was growing astronomically! In fact, there were so many people that it created a housing and food crisis; therefore, the believers held all things in common. Barnabas sold his home and gave the money to the apostles.

THE YEAR 34

ACTS 4-5

ROME AND THE EMPIRE

It was in *circa* 29 that Herod Antipas of Galilee divorced his wife. That wife was the daughter of Aretas, a prince who ruled part of Syria. Aretas was outraged. His hatred of Antipas of Galilee was beyond measure. In the year 34, Aretas had his revenge. His army moved into Antipas' province, conquered a portion of it, and kept the land. (Antipas' second wife was the one who had John the Baptist beheaded.)

ISRAEL

It was around the year 34 that Paul left Tarsus and moved to Jerusalem. It is almost a certainty that Paul lived with his blood kin, Andronicus and Junias (see Romans 16). It may have been their conversion to Christ that infuriated Paul to the point of launching out against the Christians.

It was also in one of the enclosures of the temple walls, within the temple itself, where Paul sat at Gamaliel's feet and learned the sacred Law of Moses.

Paul could not have imagined that something that happened in Syria and Galilee in 34 would almost cost his life in the year 37. It had to do with Aretas IV and Herod Antipas.

THE CHURCH

The church was in somewhat of a crisis as a result of the enormous number of people who had been saved and the foreigners who chose to stay in Jerusalem. As a result, all the believers brought their money to the apostles. (Ananias and Sapphira kept back a portion of their money. The sudden death of these two people, in the presence of Peter, stunned a city, causing even more to become believers.)

We now come to the year 35.

THE YEAR 35

ACTS 5

ROME AND THE EMPIRE

Tiberius had just two years left to live. Pontius Pilate had just one year left to reign in Judea. Antipas was chafing over having lost a small slice of Galilee at the hands of Aretas. The emperor had appointed a *legate* for Syria by the name of Vitellius. Vitellius had to restrain both Antipas and Aretas IV from a full-blown war. Vitellius was told by the emperor to keep a close eye on Judea and Jerusalem. If there was any major problem, he was to move into Judea immediately. The Jews knew this and were insulted that anyone, or anything, was a watchdog over Jerusalem.

ISRAEL

Many signs and wonders were performed by the Twelve. At this time the twelve disciples were all arrested (Acts 5:17–42).

The high priest, Joseph, son of Caiaphas (the same man who had officiated over the crucifixion of Jesus Christ and had recently arrested Peter and John), had ordered their arrest. The Twelve were brought before the Sadducees in the same place where Jesus had been tried. Gamaliel dissuaded the Council from any thoughts of execution by reminding them of a man named Theudas who, a few years earlier, had led a group of four hundred people to the Jordan River, declaring that God would part the waters of the Jordan and the four hundred would walk over on dry land. (This incident took place as part of a larger group of Jews being led by a man named Judas.) The Jordan did not open, and Theudas' followers scattered. Gamaliel counseled that the same would soon happen to the Twelve.

THE CHURCH

The Twelve were flogged, threatened, and released. The church was exuberant when they were released.

We now begin to approach the event-filled years of 36 and 37.

THE YEAR 36

ACTS 6

We mark this year as the first sign that "peaceful coexistence" with Rome was wavering.

ROME AND THE EMPIRE

Vitellius, governor of Syria, sent a report of the beating of the Twelve to Rome. Pontius Pilate, who had ruled Judea for ten years (26–36), was recalled to Rome for having ruled with too heavy a hand.

Marcellus was appointed governor of Judea (36–37) by Tiberius.

ISRAEL

The historian Josephus tells us that at this time intermittent, local, short-lived rebellions had begun. One of them took place in the year 36 in Samaria. A group of Samaritans gathered on Mount Gerizim with obvious military intent. Pontius Pilate had attacked this group of men.

THE CHURCH

At this time the church faced its first internal problem. There were two types of Jews in the church—those who were local and those who came from the Greek-speaking world. Foreign Jews were called Hellenic Jews. There was murmuring. The Hellenic Jews felt the distribution of food favored the local widows.

The Twelve, not wanting to be distracted from their ministry in the Colonade of Solomon, had the church appoint seven men to distribute the food. One of those men was the much-respected *Stephen*.

It was at this time that Stephen began to perform miracles. This was unprecedented! Stephen was not one of the Twelve! Stephen also began debating with the unbelieving Jews who gathered in the Libertine Synagogue. This was a synagogue built in Jerusalem with the money of the foreign Jews so they could have a place to meet and speak their Greek language.

Stephen and Paul would have met at the Hellenic synagogue. The stage was set in Jerusalem for the creating of a plot, trial, and death of Stephen.

So it is that we come to one of the most event-filled years of first-century Christianity... events of Christians, Romans, and non-believers, all packed into one year. It all started in March of the year 37.

THE YEAR 37

ACTS 6, 7, 8, 9

ROME AND THE EMPIRE

The year 37 is one of the three most event-filled years in the history of the church (the three years being 30, 37, and 47). The year began with the death of an emperor.

The Emperor Tiberius died on March 16 of the year 37. Word circulated in the world's marketplaces that since Tiberius was taking too long to die, Gaius Caligula helped him along by suffocating him. On March 16, Gaius Caligula was crowned emperor. Caligula was twenty-five years old, and he was quite mad. Beside him was his treacherous nineteen-year-old sister, Agrippina.

In October Caligula came down with a raging fever. Recovering in December, he emerged stark-raving mad. Tiberius, previous to his death, made the remark about Caligula, "I am raising a viper for the empire."

Tiberius was Caligula's uncle, but Caligula's real claim to the throne was that Augustus Caesar and Mark Anthony were his great-grandfathers. The people had high expectations of the great-grandson of Augustus. Everyone hoped Caligula would be another Augustus Caesar.

Even as Caligula took the throne, he began his reign with the assassination of two of his grandparents.

Caligula's sister, Agrippina, bore a son on December 15 of 37. His name was Germanicus, but he is also known by the name of Nero. He would one day rival Caligula in his perverseness and insanity. Like uncle, like nephew!

After Caligula's illness, he had everyone killed whom he suspected of trying to maneuver their way into being his successor.

For the next five years the main news heard throughout the empire was about Caligula. Hardly a month would pass but some outrageous, unbelievable news about Caligula reached the ears of the populace of the empire. It would be difficult to find anyone in human history more creative in his depravity, a greater spender of wealth, more maniacal in his treatment of those who were around him, or more delusional in his claims about himself. We will list some of the things people heard about this man, be it in Israel, Babylonia, or the German frontiers, for the next five years. This man cast a dark shadow across a shocked empire.

THE CHURCH

This is the same year that Stephen was arrested and stoned, so graphically told in Acts 6 and 7. Just after the death of Stephen, Paul was appointed the director of a sweeping persecution of Christians that covered all Israel (Acts 8:1–3; Acts 9:1, 2).

Philip's preaching in Samaria and the baptizing of the eunuch also took place in this year, as did the record of John and Peter's traveling throughout Samaria preaching the gospel.

In Jerusalem Paul gained permission not only to take his inordinate persecution of Christians to Israel, but he also gained permission to go to Syria to arrest and try believers in Damascus. From Jerusalem to Damascus: 168 miles (269 km).

In 37 Paul was struck down on the road to Damascus and then baptized by a man named Ananias. Paul entered Damascus, thereby entering the small kingdom of Aretas, and he immediately preached the gospel in a synagogue. It was there in Damascus that Paul received his first beating with thirty-nine lashes. The unbelieving Jewish leaders began plotting to kill Paul.

King Aretas had appointed a governor of the city of Damascus, referred to as a mayor. This mayor/governor cooperated with the local synagogue leaders to close the city gates in order to find and kill Paul. Instead of allowing Paul to be captured, the brothers and sisters in the church in Damascus lowered Paul in a basket through a window of one of the rooms that was built into the city wall.

It was this same year that Paul, having escaped from Damascus, came to Jerusalem to meet with Peter and James for fifteen days. Paul returned to the Libertine Synagogue,* where he had debated Stephen and saw Stephen dragged out of the synagogue and stoned. Once more a plot was hatched, but this time it was against Paul's life rather than Stephen's.

The brothers in Jerusalem took Paul to the seaport at Caesarea. From Jerusalem to Caesarea-by-the-Sea: 78 miles (125 km).

Paul then sailed north to his home in Tarsus. From Caesarea to Tarsus, Cilicia: 429 miles (690 km).† He would not be heard from again for seven years, in the year 43.

The blood-soaked year of 37 at last came to an end.

---

* Paul's second beating with thirty-nine lashes may have happened there at the Libertine Synagogue.
† Because ships traveled the shoreline, the mileage is the same whether you travel by land or by sea.

THE YEAR 38

ACTS 8-9

ROME AND THE EMPIRE

In the year 38 Caligula took a new wife named Lollia (his second wife). This was also the year that Caligula commissioned the building of two huge barges to be built on a small, one-mile lake. These two extravagant barges were so lavishly made that they *almost* single-handedly bankrupted the empire. Then on May 24, Caligula executed two men who were closest to being his rivals for the throne. He also banished several others.

It was also possibly at this time that Caligula had a solid gold statue made of himself. Each day an exact duplicate of the clothes he wore were placed on the statue. Caligula also began to think of himself as the son of Zeus. He would very soon enlarge that concept to the point that he declared he *was* in fact the real son of Zeus, and therefore a god.

There was an anti-Jewish riot in Alexandria. (It was later, in the year 65, that the Alexandrians vented their hatred of the local Jews and virtually liquidated the entire Jewish population.)

ISRAEL

In Israel Joseph, son of Caiaphas, had reigned as high priest from the year 18 to the year 37. In this year the man who had presided over the death of Jesus Christ and the whipping of the twelve apostles was finally replaced by Theophilus, son of Ananus (38–41).

THE CHURCH

In Jerusalem, the church had vanished. The apostles had been in hiding, but now they left the city and traveled the nation, strengthening the scores of new churches born overnight in Judea, Samaria, and Galilee.

Peter traveled to Joppa, preaching the gospel. Jerusalem to Joppa: 39 miles (61 km).* It was there that he raised Tabitha from the dead, and many came to believe in the Lord as a result. Peter stayed with Simon the tanner (Acts 9:36–43).

Paul was not a believer on the day Stephen died; yet, his actions of persecuting Christians had caused him to play a part in the planting of a hundred churches or more. Paul's persecution in Jerusalem had caused the apostles to finally go out into "Judea, Samaria, and Galilee" and raise up churches.

We now come to the year 39.

---

* The number of miles a person could average in a day was ten miles ... with as few as five and as many as twenty. If you calculate the time it takes to go from one point to another, we recommend you stay with the average of ten miles per day.

THE YEAR 39

ACTS 10

ROME AND THE EMPIRE

The marketplaces of the empire were beginning to hear of the strange eccentricities of their new emperor. His conduct for the next five years kept the marketplaces of the empire fully entertained.

At the age of twenty-seven, Caligula took his *fourth* wife, named Milonia. By this time the treasury of the empire was empty. What he did to keep the empire afloat financially was both savage and creative. First, he turned one wing of the palace into a brothel. Next, he forced many of the wealthy of Rome to sign over their entire inheritance to him upon their death! For some, he obliged them to die young by killing them. He confiscated gold anywhere he could find it. He found new things to tax.

Caligula built a walkway from the palace to the temple of Zeus so that he could stroll over to that temple undisturbed and there talk with his father, Father Zeus. Caligula sometimes spent hours discussing matters with a stone statue. In his deranged mind, Caligula was even heard to scream at Zeus when Zeus disagreed with him.

Perhaps the strangest thing Caligula ever did was to order the building of a pontoon bridge from Naples to Capri. He then had the pontoons covered, thereby turning them into a highway. Then, wearing the three-hundred-year-old breastplate of Alexander the Great, he mounted a stallion, crossed over into Capri and, in his sick mind, announced that he had defeated the god of the underworld (Neptune).

The entire empire was being entertained with his extreme lunacy.

In that same year he had a quarrel with the Roman Senate. He announced that he might appoint his horse as a senator. Caligula declared any jokes made about him to be an act of treason. It was also in this period of time he ordered a cousin of his to be executed because his cousin wore a robe similar to his.

It was also at this time Caligula became fascinated with stories about the mysterious room called the Holy of Holies in the temple in Jerusalem.

In Israel, men marked the audacity of Antipas when he asked Caligula to give him the title of *king*.

In just one year, Agrippa, a descendant of Herod the Great, did something no one else had done since the death of Herod the Great. Agrippa influenced Caligula to depose and exile Antipas (governor of Galilee).*

The one sane thing Caligula did during his entire reign was to leave Rome and spend a winter on the Rhine, thereby giving Rome a slight rest from his reign of horror.

While Caligula was gone, a conspiracy to assassinate him was hatched. Agrippina, Caligula's sister, ever the conniver, was discovered to have been one of those planning her brother's assassination. Despite the fact that Agrippina was with child, he ordered her executed. In the meantime, however, he came up with one more of his insane ways to

---

* Agrippa, the nephew of Antipas (and also his brother-in-law) was a friend of Caligula.

54

raise money. He forced Agrippina to be serially raped for a week, selling her to the highest bidders. At the end of that week he changed his mind about executing Agrippina and banished her instead.

A large part of the year 39 found Caligula executing those who were conspirators.

It is important to note that it was this same year that another member of the royal family wed. His name was Claudius. At age forty-nine, Claudius married his second wife, Messalina. Messalina was also the great-granddaughter of no less than Caesar Augustus. (Claudius had married his second cousin. He just missed the scandal of incest.) No one realized it, but this marriage would soon strengthen Claudius' claim to the throne.

The marketplace of the empire had much to talk about in the year 39.

ISRAEL

In the year 39 Marullus was governor of Judea. Antipas was governor of Galilee.

THE CHURCH

The nonexistent church in Jerusalem, in fact, now existed in the towns and cities of Judea, Galilee, and Samaria. All those churches were miniature duplicates of the mother church. This would be the first of three times the church in Jerusalem would close down. She would revive twice. The third time, she was destroyed forever.

An all-Jewish church had been raised up in Antioch by a handful of Jews who had fled persecution in Jerusalem. These overzealous believers also told the Gentiles of Christ. Eventually that simple event changed history.

All of this took place while the Twelve were criss-crossing Judea, Samaria, and Galilee preaching the gospel and raising up churches. Although Peter had converted and baptized Cornelius in Caesarea, no one was paying attention to the fact that at the same time, up in Antioch, Jewish brothers and sisters had begun preaching the gospel to uncircumcised heathen! The Gentiles were receiving the gospel gladly.

Then came the year 40 when Israel heard the most mortifying news in over one hundred years.

THE YEAR 40

(NOT MENTIONED IN ACTS)

ROME AND THE EMPIRE

Agrippa was officially made a *tetrarch*, ruler of Galilee. His power was limited. Theoretically, he answered only to Rome. But, in fact, it was the governor (the legate) of Syria who was the official watchdog of Agrippa and Israel.

Suddenly Agrippa was faced with the greatest challenge of his career. So was Israel. Caligula announced that he would have a statue of himself taken to Jerusalem and placed in the Holy of Holies! When this news reached Judea, an entire nation was horrified. There had already been one *Abomination of Desolation*.* The people of Israel responded. Ten thousand Jews knelt before the gates of Jerusalem, bared their necks, and vowed they would die by the sword before this statue would enter Jerusalem.

It was Agrippa who convinced Caligula to consider backing down.

It was also about this time that Caligula began forcing the wives of all the senators to "participate" in his brothel.

By now, Caligula was totally paranoid. He had every reason to be so. Thousands of the prominent citizens of Rome wanted him dead.

Now we dare to look at a future view of the emperorship which was beginning to be discussed because of the

---

* A heathen had entered the Holy of Holies.

57

unbridled, unrestrained, unchecked, uncontrolled power of emperors.

THE MAN OF SIN AND THE MAN OF LAWLESSNESS

In the mind of everyone who lived in the Roman Empire, there was no concept of succession of emperors. That is, there was simply *the emperor*. He was singular. He was one person, a personification, one man who was always there, continuing year after year, ad infinitum. It had been almost one hundred years since Julius Caesar had been assassinated and Augustus Caesar had taken the throne. From that day until Caligula—in the minds of the citizens of the world—there had been only *one* person who sat on the throne in Rome, that is, *the emperor*.

To a lesser degree, yet similarly, there is only *one* pope. We see new popes come and go, yet there is *one* pope. In Rome, there was succession, but the emperor was, in fact, a god.

Further, at no time had there ever been even one law passed which limited the emperor's power. There was no "this the emperor cannot do." There were many laws in the empire, but none of them had anything to do with the emperor. There was one unwritten law. In fact, the greatest breach of conduct of the emperor was not murder: The one unwritten law was that an emperor was not to commit incest.

Here, then, was a man who had murdered without qualms, taken people's property, exiled others, and lived in awful depravity. Here was Caligula. He was totally insane, yet outside all law. There was no guilt in him: he was the emperor. To put it another way, the emperor was a man *outside law*, the man of lawlessness.

There would one day grow up in the community a view of the emperor as "the man of lawlessness." This was a Christian reference to the reigning emperor. More specifically, *the* emperor. Later, among Christians, there would grow up the term "the man of sin." This, too, was a code word for the emperor and his deeds. What Tiberius had done, which was to live in quiet depravity on the island of Capri, Caligula had now taken to the streets. Claudius would one day do the same. In the mind of all, there was only *the* emperor, a single person who had done all this.

The day would come in the reign of Claudius when he would have a new label, one given by the Jews... an anti-messiah. He would come by that name by *earning* it.

Is it possible that this new term eventually found its way into the Christian community? Would believers then place this on Christians who later rejected the Lord and were therefore called anti-Christ?

Keep this in mind as we see all these labels begin to emerge. Later, among Jews, and even later among Christians, these terms were used as they watched their emperor living in a twilight of the bedlam of his mind.

ISRAEL

Antipas is banished. Agrippa I (grandson of Herod the Great) becomes ruler of Galilee. One year later Agrippa will be ruling all the land once ruled by Herod the Great.

So was the year 40.

It will be ten more years before the first piece of Christian literature is written.

THE YEAR 41

ACTS 11

ROME AND THE EMPIRE

Herod Antipas was still in exile. Caligula was obviously marked for assassination. On January 22 of the year 41, on his way back from one of his frequent trips to the theater, Caligula was assassinated by his own bodyguards. Some weeks later, on February 12 of that same year, Claudius,* who was at that time age forty-nine, took the throne (41–54). Messalina was his wife. She had seven years left to live. Claudius had only one heir, a son named Britannicus, who would not take the throne.

It was in the year 41 that Claudius brought his niece, Agrippina, sister of mad Caligula, out of exile.

ISRAEL

This is the year Claudius made Agrippa the ruler of Judea, Samaria, Iturea, Galilee, and all else that constituted Israel. He was also allowed to be called *king*.

THE CHURCH

Peter reports to Jerusalem about salvation coming to the Gentiles (11:1).

The Antioch church is born (11:19).†

---

* Claudius' full name was Germanicus Tiberius Claudius Caesar Britannicus. The name *Britannicus* was not added until the year 43.

† Please note it has been over ten years, and the church has had not a single page of the New Testament. In other words, the church had no Bible!!

THE YEAR 42

ACTS 11

ROME AND THE EMPIRE

Messalina had not long taken the throne beside her husband when it began to be noted that she was as much a part of the intrigue of the court as any woman had ever been.

It was also this year that Agrippa found himself outside the graces of the emperor. Agrippa had planned to rebuild and extend the walls around Jerusalem without consulting the emperor. (The spying eye of the Roman governor of Syria, north of Israel, greatly opposed Agrippa's actions.)

THE CHURCH

Rome had a new emperor, and everyone was breathing easier. The Twelve were taking the gospel throughout Israel. It was in this year that word finally reached the church in Jerusalem that the church in Antioch had unique problems. What was happening in Antioch might be unscriptural, at least not Mosaic! The brothers and sisters in Antioch, in return, wanted to know if they had done something terrible, or something wonderful. They had heard of the conversion of Cornelius. But what about the circumcision? The entire Greek side of the church was uncircumcised. More to the point, was it proper that a *church* would be a Gentile church? There were five churches that were Gentile. Were they really churches? Antioch requested that an apostle journey to Antioch and answer these questions.

The apostles responded. It was a wonderful error, one which we Gentiles must be forever grateful. The apostles decided that they were too busy. They chose a tentmaker, Barnabas, to visit Antioch instead.

The Twelve had completely misjudged what was happening. It was the year 42. It would be the year 50 before an apostle would ever see Antioch. The church in Antioch was almost totally Gentile and unlike any of the other churches. By 42, Antioch was the second largest of the churches.

Barnabas left for Antioch. From Jerusalem to Antioch: 315 miles (500 km). He decided that what he saw was better than what was in the Jewish churches in Judea, Galilee, and Samaria, and that he should take full advantage of that fact.

Barnabas had to search for Paul in Tarsus. From Antioch to Tarsus: 125 miles (200 km). After finding him, Barnabas began telling him the story of Antioch. Here was a church that was not Jewish, nor was it in the Jewish expression. Barnabas also reminded Paul that Paul had once told him that in his unique conversion, the Lord had told Paul that he was to take the gospel to the Gentiles. So it was that in that notable year, Barnabas and Paul walked along *The Royal Road* to Antioch, where Paul took his place as a brother in the church in Antioch.

That made 43 a red-letter year.

THE YEAR 43

ACTS 11

ROME AND THE EMPIRE

In the year 43, Claudius left Rome and made his way to the island of Britain. By the time he returned, Britain was conquered and was part of the empire. (Rome left Britain four hundred years later.)

Among the military men fighting in Britain was a general named Vespasian. In twenty-seven years he would be emperor.

THE CHURCH

Sometime in the year 43, a prophet arrived in Antioch predicting a worldwide famine. (We can assume the word *worldwide* meant the Roman Empire.)

The church in Antioch decided to help the church in Jerusalem. There were many poor believers, and Jerusalem was the home of three great festivals each year. Beyond that, Antioch wanted to show its oneness with Jerusalem.

THE YEAR 44

ACTS 12

The church in Antioch decided to give financial aid to the church in Jerusalem to help meet the coming needs of a famine. They chose Paul and Barnabas to deliver the aid.* When the two men arrived, they were met with shocking news. King Agrippa had made a bold move. He had arrested Peter and James.

By the time Paul and Barnabas reached Jerusalem,† James had been beheaded! Peter was awaiting execution after Passover (*circa* April).

Here are three events all happening at the same time, and Luke was telling them all at once in Acts: the church in Antioch giving aid to the church in Jerusalem, Peter facing death in Jerusalem, and the death of Agrippa at the palace in Caesarea.

At this same time, Peter was delivered out of prison by a messenger of heaven (Acts 12:1–18).

Alas, no one in the church noticed the two visitors from Antioch.

The famine struck.

Agrippa had an abundance of grain to sell to other provinces, *if* he chose to do so. Leaders from the cities of

---

* There is a reason that Luke had inserted the story of Paul and Barnabas going to Jerusalem. It goes like this: Later, in the year 49, a group of Pharisees charged that Paul had *never* been to the church in Jerusalem, that Paul was a false apostle who feared meeting the Twelve. (Paul had previously spent fifteen days with Peter, James, and John, in the year 37.)

† Nineteen days by foot, eleven days by horse, seven days by wagon, four days by ship, plus one day by foot. Approximately 315 miles (500 km).

Tyre and Sidon came to the capital city to ask Herod Agrippa's court to plead their case for grain (Acts 12:20). While they waited to see Agrippa, he prepared a speech for them. He appeared before them in a garment made of twined silver thread. Agrippa began speaking just as the morning sun broke over the wall. Agrippa was delivering a masterful oration. When the sun hit his robe, it appeared to shine like fire. Because their stomachs were riding on Agrippa's goodwill, the audience began to cry out, "This is not a man who spoke; this is the voice of a god." Herod Agrippa did not bother to give God the glory, and instead accepted the praise from the people to himself. Luke tells us that a heavenly messenger struck Agrippa and that he died of worms (Acts 12:23).

This event is not only recorded in Scripture, but it is also paralleled in the writings of the first-century historian Josephus.

As to who would replace Agrippa? Israel was distraught over the selection of that replacement. Agrippa had been *part* Jewish and familiar with the Jewish people. But to replace Agrippa, Claudius selected a Roman soldier who knew nothing about the Jewish people. This man was Fadus (44–46). Note Fadus' arrival as the year's unrest grew into resistance and, eventually, rebellion.

This disdain for a *Roman* governor would continue for twenty-two more years. Fadus would reign for only three years. After that no future governors of Israel ruled more than two years. Each governor was replaced frequently, always for their inability to bring *Pax Romana* (Roman peace) to Israel.

The famine began in the year 44 and lasted through the year 47. Paul and Barnabas, having delivered aid to the church in Jerusalem, returned to Antioch, their presence in Jerusalem having gone unnoticed.

God's gospel now spread rapidly in Israel.

Mark this: Paul had been in Jerusalem in the years 37 and 44, but future charges against him stated that he had *never* been to Jerusalem since his conversion.*

In Rome a man named Cassias was appointed the governor of Syria, still maintaining status as the watchdog of Israel.

We now move forward to the year 45, with its growing insurrection.

---

* Let the record show that at this time Paul had been beaten one time in Damascus and twice in Jerusalem. We *will* keep count.

THE YEAR 45

ROME AND THE EMPIRE

During this year, the church in Antioch continued to grow and to spread to outlying towns and cities.

In this year, Claudius returned to Rome from Britain. Claudius' wife, Messalina, charged Valerius with treason. Valerius was in charge of Rome while Claudius was away. He was forced to commit suicide. Messalina was feeling her power, an unwise choice for anyone living in Rome. (Messalina had three years left to live.)

In this year, the Greek seaport city of Dyrrachium came into prominence as the best crossing place from Greece to Italy... at a port called Brundusium. Mark that fact. It is this city that will play a major role in the history of the next fourteen hundred years!

ISRAEL

This is the year Fadus captured Theudas, the man who had, a few years earlier, led a small group of his followers to the Jordan River, announcing to them that the Jordan waters would part upon his arrival. The Jordan River did not part. Theudas was later executed. Rome did not like Jewish prophets, false or otherwise.

Once more the name Judas the Galilean is mentioned. He, too, had claimed he was the Jewish messiah. He, like Theudas, was captured and executed.

But these apocalyptic-type men would continue to appear. Their refrain was always the same—revolt against Rome and the Jewish messiah will appear.

The first piece of Christian literature is drawing near.

THE YEAR 46

ACTS 13:1

There were five men who often met for prayer in the church in Antioch. They were local prophets. (This word *prophet* simply means those who are capable of proclaiming Jesus Christ.) Some were prophets before Christ was born, proclaiming the future arrival of the Lord Jesus Christ. Some were prophets while Jesus lived on the earth, proclaiming Jesus Christ after His ascension and indwelling.

These five Antioch men moved throughout the city, proclaiming Christ. The church in Antioch was large, vibrant, vivacious, and not at all like any other church. It also changed the course of human history.

The year 46 and the line of churches coming out of Jerusalem ends. The year 47 will mark the beginning of the Antioch line of churches.

We are still four years away from the existence of the first piece of literature that will later be part of the New Testament. In other words, there are twenty-seven books of the New Testament that have not yet been written, but the background to the first one begins in the year 47. Understand the years 47–50 and you will understand that *first* piece of Christian literature.

WHAT DO WE MEAN BY *THE STORY*?

Throughout this book you find a reference to the term *The Story*. That story is made up of the unbroken events that reach from Pentecost to the destruction of Jerusalem. It is a tale which has never been known or told until now; yet, to know that story is life-changing. No one has created a model of the first-century story from 30 to 70. From this moment on, keep in mind you are seeing the merging of *The Story* and the model.

You are about to read the part of *The Story* that tells you about the letter to four churches in Galatia. You will learn what provoked Paul to write that letter.

Every Bible teacher should have a first-century model, which grows out of knowing *The Story*. Every Bible student should have a first-century model.

And now *The Story* continues.

The End of the
Jerusalem Line of Churches...
and the
Beginning of the
Gentile Line of Churches

THE END OF THE JERUSALEM LINE OF CHURCHES

The churches which came out of Jerusalem were all of one culture, one race, and one mother language. All these churches *fit* the Jewish people, its traditions, its cultures, and its rituals, as well as its deeply-ingrained prejudices.

This "way" of churches should be employed when it is confined to one country with one culture and, generally speaking, one mindset, one history, one way of doing things. It is a place where, when someone walks into a meeting, the meeting *fits* those who come in.

In Search of the Organic Church

THE SCANDAL OF AMERICAN AND BRITISH MISSIONARIES

Americans have taken the American way of doing "church" and overlaid it onto *all* other cultures.* This is not giving the world one organic church.

What is the way churches should ever be raised up?

Even the organic church is but leftover parts of the Reformation church.

What is the way churches should ever be raised up? There is the universal catholic expression of church, which is not organic. Nor is the Protestant church organic. How can the organic church be born? The Antioch line of churches tell us.

What is the lesson of the Gentile church? If you are foreign to a people, never use the Jerusalem line of churches. If you are working in a land not your own, you move to the Antioch way of planting churches.

Be advised, no one has ever dared to plant churches the way Paul raised up churches. The Antioch line of church is not only *not* for the fainthearted; it is also not dared even by the bravest of the brave.

We now begin . . .

---

* See *The Americanization of Christianity*, SeedSowers Publishing House.

BOOK II

THE ANTIOCH LINE
47-53

(The churches which came out of the
church in Antioch)

Acts 13:1–18:3

THE
ANTIOCH LINE
OF
CHURCHES

The Years 47–53

(Paul's Somewhat Insane Way of Planting Churches)*

The Antioch line of churches begins.
These are churches raised up by itinerant workers.
The worker leaves shortly after he raises up the church.
This is the organic expression of the church.

---

* To those who desire to plant churches: If you do not think Paul's way of raising up churches is not scary, then why not try it yourself?

WHAT DO WE LEARN FROM THE ANTIOCH LINE OF CHURCHES?

We learn what the church is and what she is intended to look like. We see the church in its practice. We also get a hint of her other-realm nature. The revelation of the church. How the church is to be raised up, which is a hair-raising event, to say the least.

The organic nature of the church gives us the key to how the church can be restored.

The Antioch line of churches comes into being by nature.

The ecclesia is alive; she has DNA. Help her to get started, leave her alone—without elders or anything else—and the natural expression of the church comes forth. This can only happen with an itinerant church planter who loves God, loves God's people, trusts "laymen," has *no* present-day pastor mentality, is not addicted to preaching every week and can walk off and leave the church on its own for a year or two. Such is the Antioch style.

God chose the way Paul raised up churches as the way for churches to be raised up...allowing every church to find its natural expression.

The Years 37–46 in Review

The day Stephen died, the persecution began. The believers fled Jerusalem* (Acts 6, 7, 8). Undaunted, John and Peter began preaching the gospel in Judea and Galilee, and Philip in Samaria and Ethiopia.

Then came Paul's conversion, being let out over a wall in a basket at Damascus,† and his trip to Jerusalem to meet Peter, John and James, who were in hiding in Jerusalem. Then came the years 40–42 . . . the healing at Lydda (Acts 9), the conversion of Cornelius (Acts 10), Peter's preaching to the Gentiles (Acts 10), and Peter's reporting to the twelve apostles the conversion of the Gentiles in 41 (Acts 11). Then came the birth of the church in Antioch (41–42).

All of this happened while an utterly insane, depraved monster ruled Rome.

We are now moving toward the most important event since Pentecost. What happened next, the events in Antioch, would play a major role in the move of the compass.

---

* This was the first time the church in Jerusalem ceased to exist.

† Paul was almost certainly beaten with thirty-nine lashes at the synagogue in Damascus.

Those of us who are ministers do many things we declare to be New Testament, and base it on *verse* extraction. Let us now look, not at fragmented passages, but upon the panoramic *whole*.

We are now approaching the precedent-shattering years of 47–58. When you have finished, let no man dare say, "That is the way they did it then, and we are doing it exactly the same way today."

THE BACKGROUND TO PAUL'S LETTER TO THE GALATIANS BEGINS

YEAR: 47   ACTS 13

Every time the background to one of Paul's letters begins, we will make note of it.

The events of 47–50 are what provoked Paul to write Galatians. Understand those events and those years, and you will understand the letter to the Galatians.

How do we accomplish this?

1. Luke tells us much. Keep in mind that Luke wrote Acts in the year 63, while Galatians was written in the year 50. This means Luke had read Galatians *before* he wrote Acts. Therefore, in Acts 13:1–15:40, Luke is helping us fill in the blanks surrounding and leading up to the letter to the Galatians.

2. Reading Paul's letters is like hearing one side of a telephone conversation. By inverting (mirroring) the Galatian letter we are able to learn the other half of the conversation. We will do this with every one of Paul's letters. By doing this, each letter becomes crystal clear as we read it.

THE YEAR 47

ACTS 13

The year 47 was Rome's 800th birthday. In Israel, Joseph, son of Camith, was high priest in Israel.

In the spring of 47, there was a prayer meeting in Antioch. It was an unusual prayer meeting. Some brothers were *ministering to the Lord* (Acts 13:1–4).

Five men were present: Barnabas, Paul, Lucius, Manaen, and Simeon (also called Simon the Black).

The Holy Spirit spoke to these men, "Set apart for me Paul and Barnabas for the ministry to which I have called them" (Acts 13:2). Things moved fast after that. That ministry? To take the gospel to the Gentiles.

The Antioch church was to become a bridge from being a Jewish church to becoming a Gentile church, and on to becoming a whole new kind of church.

Amazingly, those five men had no idea where Paul and Barnabas were to go in order to begin. The church sent them to the island of Cyprus to look!

PAUL'S FIRST JOURNEY

Paul's First Church Planting Journey
in the
Antioch Line of Church Planting

JOURNEY ONE

The first church planting journey began in the spring of 47.

Barnabas and Paul walked ten miles south of Antioch to the seaport town of Seleucia. From there the two men sailed to the island of Cyprus (Acts 13:4). With them was John Mark.

John Mark would one day play a major role in Paul's life, but *not* now. One day Mark would also write the book called *The Gospel According to Mark*.

Mark was on that journey because, as a child, he had witnessed the crucifixion and resurrection of Jesus Christ. We gave Mark the age of twenty-four in the year 47 (having given him the age of seven in 30). He had come to help carry the baggage of Paul and Barnabas.

One month was spent on Cyprus. It is late summer, 47.

Tradition tells us Paul and Barnabas were beaten with a whip thirty-nine times at the synagogue in Old Paphos. That would account for Paul's second of five whippings.*

At *New* Paphos, Paul preached to the governor of Cyprus (Acts 13:7–12) and blinded a Jewish reprobate. Paul also learned that the very last place the gospel had ever reached was in a small town seven miles east of Attalia in the province of Pamphylia, which was a four-day trip by ship, due north.

SHIPWRECK ONE

Now we come to what is almost certainly Paul's *first* shipwreck, during the voyage from Cyprus to Perga of Pamphylia. Paul later referred to it as "a night and a day in the sea."

---

* He may also have been scourged and then beaten at the synagogue in Jerusalem in the year 37.

Paul and Barnabas visited the small Jewish gathering in nearby Perga, and then set out on a journey which would take them four thousand feet up to a plateau called Galatia. That would be the most harrowing journey of Paul's life. (See II Corinthians 6 and following, written ten years later.)

They arrived in Galatia in late summer, *circa* 47.

Claudius was emperor. His wife Messalina had one year left to live. Alexander was the governor of Israel (46–48). Joseph of Camith was high priest.

Dates Which Should Shake Our World

The dates which you are about to read are those of the months Paul spent in each city...in other words, the short length of time spent raising up a church and then leaving it. This is the first time these dates have ever been published. This is the way churches ought to be planted. (There is no other way for a church to be *organic*.)*

---

* What you are about to see altered my life forever. May it do the same for you.

Raise up a Church, Then Leave

The first city Paul and Barnabas came to was on the edge of the province of Pisidia, named Antioch. It was distinguished from sixteen other cities by that name by being called Pisidia's Antioch (Acts 13:14–50).

Here, for the first time, a church began as a Gentile church. Luke went out of his way (34 sentences) to make that point. Despite the fact this church was raised up by two men who were Jews and were steeped in Jewish tradition, ritual and custom, the church would have a non-Jewish way of expressing itself.

Here we see the amazing way of church planting, first-century style.

Paul *arrived* in Pisidia . . . . July, 47
Paul *departed* from Pisidia . . . . November, 47
   Total time spent in Pisidia . . . . . . 5 Months

No building, no New Testament, no Christian presence nearby, no Bible teaching—just God's people, the church, and an indwelling Lord.

With enemies in Pisidia, Paul then moved on to Iconium, where once more he encountered inflexible religion (Acts 14:1–6).

Paul *arrived* in Iconium . . . . December, 47
Paul *departed* from Iconium . . . . April, 48
   Total time spent in Iconium . . . . . 5 Months

Will this become a pattern?
Paul left Iconium and moved on to the city of Lystra.

THE YEAR 48

ACTS 14

We now come to the year 48 and two more Gentile churches. The *third* church was Lystra (Acts 14:8–20).

Paul *arrived* in Lystra . . . . May, 48
Paul *departed* from Lystra . . . . August, 48
   Total time spent in Lystra . . . . . . 4 Months

There is no mention in Luke's account, but one very important person was saved in Lystra. *That convert was Timothy*. We estimate Timothy was age twenty. Timothy would become one of *eight* Gentile church planters, more or less the equivalent of the Twelve.

Paul was stoned at Lystra. He left Lystra and went to Derbe (Acts 14:19–20). Derbe would be the last of four churches Paul raised up in Galatia. One of the converts that September was Gaius of Derbe. Gaius would also become one of those *eight* workers. We give Gaius the age of twenty-five in the year 48.

Paul *arrived* in Derbe . . . . September, 48
Paul *departed* from Derbe . . . . December, 48
   Total time spent in Derbe . . . . . . 4 Months

Is doing this really possible?

A Personal Word about the Unutterable Challenge of Planting Churches

When I read what you have just read, I was astonished! A church, from a dead start... and five months later, left... in a world where Christ was unknown. This flies in the face of all our present-day thinking or understanding. No church buildings, no Bibles, no Bible study, no previous knowledge of Jesus Christ. Could this be done, using today's evangelical capacities?

From the time Paul entered a city until the time he left a fledgling church, he was there no longer than a *maximum* of four or five months. Further, these Galatians were the poorest in the empire. They were virtually all illiterate. They were social outcasts in their cities. Only five months! All were new Christians. Paul left them!

Remember, you and I have long ago been taught that literacy, the ability to read the New Testament, is synonymous with being a Christian.

More astounding was that Paul not only left Galatia, but would not return for over a year.

Is there anyone alive who could do this?

I pushed back my chair, and said out loud, "There is nothing like this practice anywhere in modern-day Christianity."

For the next seven years I did everything in my power to find the secret to how Paul did this. What was the key? No such ministry existed which dared plant churches this way.

As one who has now spent half my life planting churches by this Pauline way, one thing becomes obvious: There needs to be a great deal of *spiritual* help given, as well as a great deal of *practical* help.

Should men pursue this way of planting churches in today's world, we would have to lay aside virtually everything about our understanding of what are the central ingredients which make up "the Christian life." It must be raised to a far higher level.

There is one lesson above all else: Jesus Christ never intended for the Christian life to be lived on so low a level as it is today. We will discover the utter inadequacies of evangelical Christianity. As an example, evangelical Christianity never uses Paul's way of church planting. If it should dare to do so, it would probably fail because of our spiritual shallowness. Paul's ministry had a spiritual depth to it which we evangelicals are not aware. It was that depth of Christ that caused Paul's churches to survive and flourish. The solo Christian life will not work. All the books in all the Christian bookstores will not cause the Christian faith to work when it is not corporate. All we do, say, write, or think is aimed at the individual Christian. In the first century, a Christian's life was a *corporate* Christian life. The outliving of the present idea of the individual Christian life is a study in futility. The Christian adventure is a corporate adventure. The living of the Christian life does not work well any other way.

At this juncture in my life, I have written thirty books. If God gives me grace and life, I will write another thirty, all of which are driven by one function: that Jesus Christ be central and the church be raised up to have an organic expression. An organic expression of the church cannot be accomplished unless the one who plants that church leaves the church on its own. She alone finds "organic." With this "bare bones" approach comes the potential to discover that the Christian life is *corporate*, not *individual*, and her local expression is unique...unlike any other!!

Is this scary? It is *very* scary. Is it difficult? It is *extremely* difficult. Is it impossible? No! What is difficult is to find men whose lives are like unto Paul's...which is close to nonexistent! Yes, it takes a great deal of itinerant practical help and a church with an awesome spiritual life, but it is not only possible, it is *God's way* of doing.

The idea of pastors standing in the pulpit and preaching to a mute audience pales into nonexistence in the presence of *the story*.

One of the most beautiful things is that once God's people see these things, *they* attempt them. We have vastly undersold the "layman's" ability to do great things, *without* a clergy present.

WHY HAVE THESE THINGS NOT BEEN SEEN BEFORE?

Why has this story not been seen before? The answer is simple. It is because never in all the history of the Christian faith have we been looking at the word of God *chronologically*. We read the New Testament in the order in which it was first handed to us. This jumbled arrangement prevents us from ever seeing the whole landscape; hence, we never see the story from beginning to end. Once we do, this beautiful, three-dimensional canvas emerges.

Let us now continue on our three-dimensional journey.

THE MARKETPLACE WAS
THE NEWSPAPER

Every city, town, and village had a marketplace. That marketplace was where *everyone* received their news. This book tells you much of what was heard in those marketplaces. But the years 37–41 and 47–49 were especially filled with spectacular news.*

---

* Israel had its most spectacular news in 57–58 and 65–70.

THE YEAR 48 CONTINUES

What happened in Galatia in the years 47 and 48 is life-changing for us who live in our age and are seeking to return to first things. Those in Rome and Israel, however, knew nothing of these two years which shook the world.

In the marketplaces of Israel, there was much talk about a man by the name of Judas and his two sons, all from Galilee. After Judas was captured by the Roman governor, he was brought to trial. The high priest ordered Judas and some of his followers to be crucified. Did this reach the ears of Paul and Barnabas while they were in Galatia? Yes. Synagogues were a telegraph of news from Israel. You can be sure they heard of it!

The year 48 was the most restless year in Israel since they had been conquered back in 86 B.C. by Pompeii. Armed clashes with Roman soldiers had begun.

The name of Agrippa II was being introduced. He was given a small section of Judea to rule.

THE FURY OF A GESTURE

During one of the annual feasts, a Roman soldier, high up on one of the towers overlooking the temple, made an obscene gesture to the Jews below. The Jews were indignant. This started a fiery dispute which would not be resolved for several years. The Jews demanded that the man be punished. It became a *cause célèbre*.

CUMANUS

The governor, Thadus, had been replaced by a new governor named Cumanus (48–49). Cumanus proved to be even more dishonest than Thadus. Because of the growing unrest, Cumanus was forced to bring in more Roman soldiers to Jerusalem, causing some Jews to react violently. These Jews were ruthlessly crushed by Cumanus. Panic in Jerusalem broke out. A number of innocent people were killed.

The tension of 48 grew even greater when some of the angry Jews plundered a caravan carrying supplies for the Roman soldiers. (This took place in Beth-horon in the province of Judea.) The soldiers, in turn, plundered Beth-horon and then arrested the officials of that city.

THE BURNED TORAH

Tension soared when one of the Roman soldiers grabbed a Torah, ripped it to pieces, and then burned it, the ultimate blasphemy. Rebellion against Rome was still eighteen years away, but in 48 it looked like it could happen at any moment.

Josephus wrote of the years 48 through 52, "These were the last years of passive resistance against Rome." Henceforth, there would be planned *and* violent resistance to Roman occupation.

It was then that the Hebrews began repeating again and again the story of the Maccabees. The Maccabees had fought against the ruling Syria (*circa* 30 B.C.), and even freed the Jewish nation from the Syrian conquerors. Something was added to that story: "If *we* will but revolt against Rome, the *messiah* will appear and he will overthrow Rome."

In the year 49 one Jew would test that theory.

Eventually, Cumanus ordered the soldier who burned the Torah beheaded.

In this tense situation, we also find our two church planters making plans to return home to Antioch from Galatia. The year 48 held one more shock.

AN ENTIRE WORLD WAS STUNNED AT THE PUBLIC EXECUTION OF THE EMPRESS

Messalina (wife of Claudius, the emperor) had committed adultery and had publicly flaunted that fact. Claudius then did something that had never been done before. Claudius ordered the empress, Messalina, to be publicly executed. This was unprecedented! Paul's view of the concept reached a new low. Paul said "without law!"

A MAN OUTSIDE THE LAW

Keep in mind, from the view of the people of the empire, the man who lived in the palace in Rome was always just one ever-perpetual person, not a series of men. Paul was aware of an emperor's perpetuity, and that this man Claudius was depraved and evil, a man of utter sin, and totally outside all law. (There was absolutely not a single law concerning the emperor.) The emperor banished men and women at any whim, confiscated others' wealth and property, and often murdered them to make the process of seizing the property happen more quickly. Now the emperor had publicly executed the empress, no trial, no permission needed, but instead, totally unrestrained by any law! Paul, like all the rest of the citizens of the empire, had watched the emperor engage in history's greatest debauchery, torture, public depravity, and sheer madness. In Paul's eyes, what Claudius would do in the years 49, 50, and 51 would forever seal that view.

Let us never forget what happened in Galatia in 47 and 48. Counterwise, let us try hard to forget what happened in Israel and Rome at that same time.

THE YEAR 49

ACTS 14-15

Now comes the behemoth year of 49. If the public execution of the empress in 48 was shocking, the year 49 was even more so.

Paul and Barnabas had been away from their home church, Antioch, for two years. In the spring of 49, they took a ship from Pamphylia to Antioch. Paul did not know the four innocent churches they had raised up would soon have a reign of fire fall on them. Nor did Paul know that in the year 49, there would take place an incident which would devastate the entire Jewish world.

A SHORT FAREWELL VISIT

After deciding to return home, Paul and Barnabas decided to make a short visit back to each of the churches in Galatia.

THE CHURCHES WERE REVISITED ACTS 14:21, 22

Paul revisited each Galatian church for about two weeks to four weeks. This revisit, including travel, lasted less than four months.

After being with Derbe for four months, the two men then retraced the dangerous trip down to Pamphylia.

THE REVISIT

Paul stayed:
One month with Lystra — January, 49

One month with Iconium — February, 49
One month with Pisidia — March, 49
Down to Perga, Pamphylia — April, 49

The four young Galatian churches would have peace for a little less than one year.

Just before they boarded a ship there in Pamphylia, bound for Syria, let's look at . . .

AMAZING FACTS

The church in Pisidia was seventeen months old.
Pisidia had not seen Paul and Barnabas in fourteen months.

The church in Iconium was thirteen months old.
Iconium had not seen Paul and Barnabas in eight months.

The church in Lystra was eight months old.
Lystra had not seen Paul and Barnabas in four months.

The church in Derbe was *only* four months old.
And now left alone!!
The church in Derbe had just bid Paul goodbye.
Derbe would not see Paul again for well over a year.

Can a four-month-old church survive being left all alone for some fourteen months . . . and face an impending attack from the outside which would sink *any* church? We *will* know the answer. It is summer of 49 by the time Paul leaves Galatia. It will be spring of 50 before we know the answer to those two questions!

Now, our first reality check. Have you seen any pews, pulpits, sermons, Bible schools, or pastors so far? Or any other present-day "biblical" trappings?

What we do today may be founded on a web of verses, but when we see the total landscape of Century One, none of the present-day practices ever appear.

Paul and Barnabas reached their home in Antioch* in about May of 49. In Antioch he would soon face an unbelievable crisis.

This is church planting—first-century style. Where are those who will try it?

This also is the pattern the Lord has given us.

This is Century One church planting! Where are the adventurous, the daring, the pioneers? It is to you this book is written.

REPORT TO ANTIOCH
SPRING 49
ACTS 14:27

Paul the church planter had been away from Antioch for two years (spring of 47–spring of 49). The report he and Barnabas gave to the church was electrifying. We note that in that same meeting were two young men who will play a major role in the first-century story. One was a physician and future historian. The other was a man named after the Titans. One was Luke, the other, Titus.

After the excitement died down, Paul and Barnabas returned to being "just brothers" in the assembly.

Finally, news of what these two had done reached the attention of the church in Jerusalem.

Peter decided to visit this wonder called *the church in Antioch*. Peter must have been greeted with awe. Barnabas

---

* In the future, Paul would report to the church in Jerusalem *before* reporting home to Antioch.

finally gave his report to Peter. (Sent to Antioch in 43, Barnabas reported to Peter in 49.) But there were men who heard the news of Antioch and Galatia, and the question they wanted to ask was, "Had those unclean, unwashed, unholy Gentiles in Galatia been *circumcised?*"

THEN CAME THE PHARISEES TO ANTIOCH!

Back in Israel there was a growing sense that many Jews were too *Roman* and that other Jews were forsaking the foundation built by Moses.

In the midst of this, *the thorn* arrived in Antioch. Legalists, traditionalists, and conformists, with their religious enslavement to their doctrines, were now to be overlaid onto the Gentile believers.

These Judean visitors did not like what they saw in Antioch: uncircumcised Gentiles excitedly in love with Jesus! That was not all. They heard there were four more Gentile churches somewhere in an obscure place called Galatia.

Now enters a man as committed to Moses as Paul was to Christ. He was a first-class villain. He was a Pharisee of Pharisees. He came with a group of fellow Pharisees from Jerusalem—with a letter in hand from James, the brother of Jesus, the Christ! Those "brothers" wanted to discover if Paul was a betrayer of Moses. These men may also have had one eye cast toward Peter. After all, Peter had stayed with Gentiles in the city of Joppa!

Antioch was very impressed with these new visitors. The church, meeting in innumerable houses, could hardly wait to have these stern-looking gentlemen in their meeting. Among them was a man whom Paul would one day call a *thorn*.

Meanwhile, in the midst of this came the shock to end all shocks ... and it probably took place during the Jerusalem Council.

A RIOT IN ROME
ONE OF THE GREAT EVENTS
OF THE DECADE

In late 49 some Jews decided to test the theory, "If we but revolt, the messiah* will appear." Ever since the *Babylonian captivity* (578 B.C.) the Jews had believed strongly in the possibility of a delivering messiah. This messiah would rescue God's people from all their enemies, including Rome.

The Romans had a tradition regarding rebels: "Start a riot, and be crushed!" If a nation rioted, the army would invade and rule with an iron heel. Live in peace with Rome; pay taxes and live in peace (*pax Romana ... unless* there was resistance). A riot was the ultimate sin.

Some twenty thousand Jews lived in Rome. Virtually all lived in a district called Trans-Tiber (across the Tiber River). A very charismatic Jew convinced a handful of Jews in Trans-Tiber that if they revolted right there in Rome, the Jewish messiah would appear and Rome would be conquered. The emperor himself was thunderstruck at such audacity.

---

* Whenever we use the word *Messiah*, indicating the Lord Jesus Christ, it will be capitalized. When we refer to the ancient Jewish teaching of a coming messiah, which has been part of their tradition for a thousand years, we will not capitalize the word *messiah*.

Claudius acted quickly. He reactivated an old, forgotten law which stated no Jews could live in Rome. Suddenly every Jew in Rome was told to leave Rome.

When the world of the Jews heard this (in the market-places of the empire), the Jews were equally horrified. So was born the term "Claudius is anti-messiah." Just the year before, Claudius had publicly executed his wife. Now in 49, he had expelled the Jews. Just as bad, Claudius had married his niece, Agrippina. Their marriage was an act of incest. In the Jewish mind, the emperor—this corporate human (a component of Tiberius, Caligula, and Claudius) was a depraved man gone mad, above the law, the personification of sin, now opposed to the messiah, *and* living in incest!

The emperor was the man of sin, the man of lawlessness, and the anti-Jewish messiah, and had *now* made twenty thousand homeless wanderers. Rage among the Jews knew no boundaries. On the other hand, the people of the empire, being good followers of the emperor, renewed their dislike of those strange Hebrews.

Paul must have felt the same attitude as all Jews. After all, Paul had two great dreams. One was to raise up a church in Rome, now made impossible by Claudius, the other to raise up Gentile workers.

Please take note:

The question has often been asked, "Who started the Christian church in Rome?" From the year 49 onward, there would be no Jewish Christians in Rome. Previously, if there had ever been even the smallest gathering of believers in the imperial city, that gathering had come to an end. But to Paul, there must be a "church in Rome," and it would be a Gentile church. The only question was how to do that without any Jewish Christians, including Paul, to take the gospel of the church to Rome.

The years 47, 48, and 49 have been filled with Himalayan events. The year 50 will match every one of those years.

We stand on the edge of the action-packed year 50, with drama to spare.

The year 50 would bring a return to the Galatian churches, Paul's second journey; Paul's brutal beating in Philippi; Paul's being thrown out of three churches; and two more of Paul's letters being written soon after.

GALATIANS
WRITTEN IN THE SPRING
OF THE YEAR 50
(ACTS 15; GALATIANS 1 AND 2)
THE WRITING OF THE WORLD'S
FIRST PIECE OF
CHRISTIAN LITERATURE

No one can be more unhappy than a religious legalist. Those Pharisees visiting Antioch were miserable!

Luke tells us of their arrival (Acts 15), yes, but it takes the reading of the letter to the Galatians, Chapters 1 and 2, to discover what really happened. Remember, Peter was in Antioch when these glum Pharisees arrived.

By comparing the first sentences in Chapter 15 of Acts with Galatians 2:11, you discover the entire story of that visit in Antioch.*

---

* Anyone who has studied much history will find that it is always difficult to wrap your mind around one particular problem: that the writer will be telling you about an event which took place in one particular year, yet writing about it years later. This is the situation we face here. Luke had read Galatians long *before* he wrote Acts 15.

Luke tells us about an event which took place in the early part of the year 50 (Acts 15:1), but Luke *wrote* this story, *circa 63*! Try, then, to keep in mind that when Luke wrote what happened in Antioch with those Pharisees in the year 50, he was actually writing Acts thirteen years later!

Voila!

REMEMBER:
Luke had long since read the Galatian letter
before he wrote Chapter 15 of Acts!

When we look at Galatians 1 and 2, keep in mind that Luke had read those same words many years earlier. Then he wrote about them. Consequently, Luke found no reason to repeat the Paul/Peter/Pharisees episode in Acts.

By combining Galatians 1 and 2 with the opening passage of Acts 15, we are able to weave together a full picture of what took place when all those Jerusalem visitors—and Peter—dropped in on the church in Antioch.

PETER REBUKED
GALATIANS 2:11–21
ACTS 15

Peter was joyfully received in Antioch. We can be sure many were healed. While among the Gentiles, Peter ate, touched, and fellowshipped with the heathen and behaved in very "gentilish" ways.

Then came those very unhappy legalists. These Judeans were horrified that Jews and Gentiles were eating together, touching one another, and mingling with one another.

At what next appears to be a goodbye banquet for Simon Peter, came drama.

Peter entered the room. Then came in the legalists. (They had been telling the Gentiles they had to be circumcised in order to be saved.) There was tension enough in the room. Peter saw the visitors sitting together, being served kosher food at the hands of Jewish cooks. Peter wavered. He sat with the legalists. Barnabas walked in. He wavered. Then Paul walked in. The year 50 was born! So was Chapter 2 of Galatians.

In my mind's eye I see...

Paul standing a good distance from Peter. In a loud voice Paul began rebuking Peter (Galatians 2.) What happened was a tale for the telling for years to come. An apostle had rebuked the *chief* apostle and was unapologetic about it! Paul began his outburst. As he spoke, he walked toward Peter. "Why would you force Gentiles to be placed under obedience to the Law which we ourselves cannot and never have been able to obey?" The Jerusalem visitors were mortified. The Antiochians were equally stunned. Peter had been rebuked in *public*! Each time I have read this story, I have seen Paul sitting down with the Gentiles and thundering, "Someone pass the pork!"

We can be sure that the farewell banquet broke up right then. What state of mind Peter was in, we do not know, as he returned home to Jerusalem. The issue at hand was unresolved.

THE SURPRISE TWIST

Something unique happened among the legalists there in Antioch. They did *not* all go home to Jerusalem. Some decided to take a look at those four churches in Galatia. Paul did not know this. Neither did Peter. Did *thorn* go to Galatia? Methinks!

A REVELATION COMES FROM THE CHURCH IN ANTIOCH

The church in Antioch was now faced with a dilemma. Paul tells us that someone in the church in Antioch had a revelation (Galatians 2). We can assume that revelation was, "This problem came to us from Jerusalem, and it should be resolved in Jerusalem."

Meanwhile, a group of Pharisees (who had witnessed Paul rebuking Peter) were on their way to Galatia. Paul, Barnabas, and Titus* went to Jerusalem to confront Peter, et al. "Is circumcision necessary to salvation?"

Why Titus? We do not know. He was obviously held in high regard, probably because he was so much a Greek that he even *looked* uncircumcised.

THE PLOT TO DESTROY THE FOUR GENTILE CHURCHES IN GALATIA HAVE WE MET PAUL'S *THORN IN THE FLESH*?

Let us say there were *six* legalists bound for Galatia. Their purpose: Convert the Galatians to circumcision *and* ruin Paul's reputation. Failing that: Destroy the four churches

---

* We will give the age of twenty-five to Titus.

by any means necessary. It was a long journey, thereby giving these men plenty of time to plot what they were going to say when they arrived in Galatia. As they traveled, they drew up a list of charges against Paul. They also knew they would be warmly received. The letter from James would guarantee that.

Keep in mind, these Judaizers had no idea Paul was on his way to Jerusalem to confront the apostles, nor did they know Paul had made two previous trips to the Jerusalem church. "I was not known by face to the church in Jerusalem, but had been there twice."

He *was* known by face to Peter, James, and John.

Upon arrival in Derbe, the nearest city, these unhappy men charged that Paul was not only a *man-pleaser* but also a *coward*.

On what did they base these charges?

1. Paul did not tell the Gentiles about *the knife* (circumcision), with its pain and fever!
2. Paul had never been to the church in Jerusalem, nor met the Twelve; therefore, he was a self-proclaimed, *renegade* apostle.
3. Paul had persecuted the church in the year 37 (leaving the impression that Paul had never repented of that persecution).
4. Paul did not have the blessing of the mother church in Jerusalem, nor its elders.
5. They painted Paul as uneducated: Paul who had preached a false gospel.

The conclusion:

"You have been lied to and duped by Paul. You are *not* saved; you must undergo the pain of the knife."

Worst of all, they told in horror that Paul, a false apostle, had publicly *rebuked Peter*! (Please note that *only* Peter had been rebuked ... not the other Jewish Christians with Peter.)

All this pretty well destroyed the Galatian saints.

(Note: Gaius was in the church in Derbe when these men arrived.)

We do not have to wonder what happened when these Pharisees arrived in Derbe. Gaius watched these strangers rip Paul's reputation to shreds. We would not be far from the mark in believing the Lord's people were in tears.

The Judaizers came to Lystra, and then a twenty-year-old kid stepped into the arena. His mother Eunice and his grandmother Lois must have taught him in grace, as it was obvious that Timothy knew the difference between legalism and grace when he heard these visitors speak. Timothy confronted these men and, apparently, followed them to Iconium and Pisidia. These educated-by-the-book Pharisees must have been chagrined at the audacity of Timothy. Nonetheless, they did great damage to Paul's standing among the believers.

Would the four churches in Galatia ever trust Paul again? Would they even survive? Poor Derbe was only four months in Christ when Paul left and was no more than sixteen months out of heathendom upon the arrival of these legalists in the spring of 50.

(Note: No one in Jerusalem and no one in Antioch knew these destroyers were in Galatia.)

THE COUNCIL IN JERUSALEM

At the same time that havoc was occurring in the Galatian churches, Paul and Barnabas were in Jerusalem telling the

Galatian story. The reaction of the believers—pure joy. (This was the first time Jerusalem believers had ever seen Paul's face.) Paul and Barnabas' report was received with awe.

Once more, keep in mind, no one in that room knew the Pharisees were attempting to destroy Gentile Christianity. Also keep in mind, Paul was in Jerusalem while the Pharisees were stating that he had never *been* to Jerusalem.*

James, the brother of Jesus, ended the debate. A letter would be sent to Antioch. All those in the room would sign it, stating circumcision was not necessary for salvation. It would become the most famous letter in history. Somewhere down at the bottom of the signatures, in small print, was that of Titus.

Paul, Barnabas, and Titus returned to Antioch, with John Mark in tow, along with Judas (not Iscariot) and Silas as witnesses to the events in Jerusalem.

Please notice that the letter was sent *from* the church in Jerusalem, its elders, and the apostles. The letter *to* Antioch addressed no elders (Acts 15:23–30).

The Judaizers, now leaving Galatia, returned to Jerusalem. It was spring of the year 50.

We would not be far off the mark to believe it was at this time, with Titus and John Mark swapping stories and asking questions, that Mark began to *consider* writing a biography of Jesus Christ. (In five years Mark would do just that.)

THE SPLIT BETWEEN
TWO CHURCH PLANTERS

Judas and Silas were about ready to return to Jerusalem. Paul and Barnabas decided to revisit the four churches in

---

* This is actually Paul's *third* trip to Jerusalem.

Galatia, still not knowing the Judaizers had been in Galatia. Barnabas wanted to revisit Cyprus *and* also have John Mark join them again. Paul was emphatically against such a suggestion! The two men had a very strong falling out.

PRELUDE TO PAUL'S *SECOND* JOURNEY LATE SPRING, 50 (ACTS 15:36)

Paul kept on "insisting" that Mark not go with them. Barnabas, therefore, took Mark* to Cyprus. But it was Paul who kept the Jerusalem letter!

At this moment, Paul received news from Galatia. The Judaizers who had been in Antioch had also gone to Galatia!† Paul also learned what the Pharisees had said against him.

Paul was furious!

He grabbed his pen and wrote a letter to Galatia. You will find anger in every sentence in the first two chapters. Interestingly, Paul did not know the names of those Pharisees, but he *did* know how deep was the damage the church had experienced.

---

* According to the age we gave Mark (seven in the year 30), he is now twenty-seven.

† These men traveled 253 miles, all because of circumcision!

THE
LETTER
TO THE
GALATIANS

The First Piece of Christian
Literature Ever Written
Late Spring, 50
Acts 15:40

Pause here, dear reader. Make a note at Acts 15:40 as that is where the letter to the four churches in Galatia was written.

Keep in mind the background to Galatians is 47–50. Understand the events of those four years and you will understand Galatians!

Stop here and read Paul's letter to the four Galatian churches!*

---

* In today's evangelical Christianity, virtually everything in Paul's letters is applied to the individual. Please keep in mind that this totally misses the mark. Everything Paul said in Galatians was written to a body of people. The Galatian letter should be treated that way. It is to be applied primarily to a church—to a church living in community. That is how Galatians was written; that is how Galatians should be applied.

THINGS TO REMEMBER ABOUT THE GALATIAN LETTER

Galatians is the first piece of Christian literature ever written. Galatians preceded the actual penning of the four Gospels!* There is so much in Galatians to help us understand Christ, the church, et al. Galatians is fundamental to our understanding of the entire Christian faith.

It had been twenty years since Pentecost. The church had been *twenty years* without even one page of a New Testament. Now in the year 50, the kingdom of God received exactly *six pages* of what would later become the New Testament. Here is a point we overlook: The church of Jesus Christ did not have a New Testament! Never in Century One did the Christians have the twenty-seven books of the New Testament.†

But did they not get a New Testament before the end of the century? That is not the right question. The question is: *When* did the New Testament begin to be gathered together? By 100? By 200? No, not even in 250 was there "gathered together" a complete New Testament... not until after A.D. 330. There was a twenty-seven-book New Testament during the reign of the Emperor Constantine (303–336).

Please note, Paul's first letter was Galatians; but in your New Testament table of contents, Romans is listed as Paul's

---

* Mark, Matthew, Luke, and John cover the story of the years 26–30, but the first three books were actually written *circa* 55, 58, 63, and John either *circa* 70 or 90.

† You can calculate that the books of the New Testament were being written on the average of one every two years.

first letter, with Galatians fourth. Galatians is *first* and should be listed so in the New Testament!

The present arrangement must change. Otherwise, we will *never* understand the New Testament.

THE UNIQUENESS OF THE GALATIAN LETTER

The first piece of Christian literature was for *Gentiles.*

This is the first window we have into the Christian faith in its earliest years.* Immerse yourself in Galatians. You will discover that the church was central to the life of Paul, central to the early apostles, and central to the Christian's life in Antioch and Galatia. The church was community. There was also *commerce* between those four churches. The saints in each church kept up with the others, strengthened one another, and engaged in ministry to and from one another.

Above all else, dear reader, take note: That letter was *to* a church, *for* a church, *applicable* to the church, and *penned* by a church planter. There were elders in the four churches in Galatia, but not one of them was ever mentioned.† You will look in vain for any reference to elders!

Our present-day concept of the Christian life is that of the *individual* Christian. In this most primitive of all Christian writings, the entire understanding of the Christian life was centered around the church. Their Christian life was

---

* In this letter we are first introduced to grace, the Holy Spirit, Christian freedom, freedom from legalism, and the place of Moses in the life of us Gentiles. But above and beyond all this, we also get a glimpse into what "church" *meant.*
† We will later discover there were many of the Gentile churches which did not have elders.

lived by means of the church's *corporate* nature. Despite the terrible crises the four churches had passed through, the letter was written to all God's people. There is not a single reference to elders (Galatians 1:2a).

It is very clear that we cannot live the Christian life *alone*. We are like those who would attempt to obey the Law. We discover that we are too weak to live up to the demands of the Christian life on our own. You or I cannot make a very good Christian. The Christian life cannot be lived as it ought to be lived when it is independent, but only through the *inter*dependence of brothers and sisters . . . *in the assembly.*

DID TITUS DELIVER THE GALATIAN LETTER?

Here we have a mystery. In the letter to the Galatians, there is a mention of Titus. How could the Galatians know Titus' name if he had not gone to Galatia? The letter arrived ahead of Paul. Does this mean Titus had delivered the letter?

When Paul finished writing the Galatian letter, he was not sure *anyone* in Galatia would even believe him or receive him. Such was the wreckage wrought by the Pharisees. Perhaps his reputation had been destroyed. Perhaps he would arrive in Derbe and be rejected. If so, then telling them about a letter from Jerusalem which they had never seen would mean nothing to them. But if he arrived in Derbe with the letter in hand and first told the story of what happened in Jerusalem, then he, like any good military man, would have something in reserve, the Jerusalem letter.

Paul made no mention of the Jerusalem letter when he wrote to the Galatians. He would pull it out in the presence of any lingering doubters. But he did send someone ahead of him. This someone would have been with him in Jerusalem with the apostles. This man's name would also have to appear on that letter... Titus.

There were two letters. Paul's was sent to Galatia prior to his arriving. The other was carried by Paul himself... the spectacular letter from the church in Jerusalem.

It therefore came to pass that Titus arrived in Derbe in the autumn of 50.* Titus told the believers firsthand what had happened in Jerusalem. Titus also told them Paul was totally backed by the Twelve, and that Paul and Silas would arrive in a few days with the letter from Jerusalem. (*And* its signatures!) By the time Titus had finished telling his story, the church in Derbe had accepted Paul again.

We are on the precipice of Paul's second journey. Remember that at this time no Jews were allowed in Rome. There was also a city in Greece where no Jews were allowed. There is a connection, as we shall see.

---

* From Antioch to Derbe is approximately 253 miles (405 km).

140

THE BACKGROUND

TO

I THESSALONIANS

BEGINS HERE

Acts 15:40–18:1

The Years 50–51

1. Luke tells us about the events that led to Paul writing this letter. (Remember that Luke wrote Acts long after he read I Thessalonians, so he was helping us understand the events surrounding this letter.)

2. By inverting or mirroring I Thessalonians, we learn the other half of the conversation and what took place before Paul wrote this letter.

The countdown begins to I Thessalonians. In one-and-one-half years, Paul will write the second book of the New Testament!*

PRINCIPLE

Understand those one-and-one-half years and you *will* understand that second letter. It just happens that way. Why? Because the reason Paul wrote that next letter was provoked by the events which took place in that one-and-one-half years. In that time, Paul will plant the churches in Philippi, Greece and in Thessalonica...and write his first letter to the church in Thessalonica.

---

* Look in the table of contents of your Bible and you will see I Thessalonians listed as the eighth letter written by Paul, when in fact it was his second!!

THE YEAR 50

ACTS 16-17

Paul (and Silas) left Antioch, walking overland, arriving first in Derbe,* and then visiting each of the other three churches. At that time, Paul had been away from the four churches for fourteen months.

THE AGES OF THE FOUR GALATIAN CHURCHES SUMMER OF 50

Pisidia's Antioch	2 years, 8 months
Iconium	2 years, 4 months
Lystra	2 years, 1 month
Derbe	1 year, 5 months

Notice how young these four churches were, yet Paul visited each one for only a few weeks.

Taking Timothy† of Lystra with them, Paul and Silas set out for parts unknown (summer of 50). Paul had no idea where to go.

It is here that *The Story* first mentions a young man named Timothy. We must remember that two years earlier, Paul had entered Lystra, preached the gospel there, and raised up a church. At that time, Paul had met a twenty-year-old half breed whose name was Timothy. His mother's

---

* From Antioch to Derbe is 253 miles (405 km).

† Take note of Timothy. We will meet him later when Paul trains seven other young men in Ephesus.

name was Eunice and his grandmother's name was Lois. Impressed with this young man who had boldly confronted the Judaizers, Paul invited Timothy to join him on his second journey.

There is already a young man who has crossed Paul's path, and that is the remarkable Titus of Antioch. Is it possible that just about now Paul has begun thinking of a day when he would train some young men to take his place? If so, he already has three possible candidates whom he would consider: Timothy, Titus, and Gaius. There will be on this second journey three more men to add to this list.

THE SECOND JOURNEY FINDS ITS DIRECTION

The Holy Spirit had forbidden Paul from going east to Bithynia. Paul went to Troas. There in Troas, Paul had a vision. Essentially, a man in the vision said, "Come over to Europe (northern Greece) and help us" (Acts 16:9–11).

We could make a strong case that the *man* in the vision was actually a *woman* (Lydia!). Unknown to Paul, God was inviting Paul to a beating with rods, a jailing, and beyond Philippi, the hatred of the citizens of two more cities.

Did Paul know Philippi was in every way Roman, and not Greek, thereby making it a very unusual city?

THE UNIQUENESS OF PHILIPPI

On March 15, of the year 44 B.C., Julius Caesar was assassinated by Brutus and Cassius. Their army faced the army of Octavian and Mark Anthony near Philippi. It was crucial to both sides to have the city of Philippi on their side.

Philippi backed Octavius and Mark Anthony. Cassius and Brutus were defeated. Mark Anthony made Philippi a *Roman* province.

From that time onward, the Philippians were fanatical emperor zealots. They made Latin, *not* Greek, the language of the city. Philippi was an Italian-speaking city in the middle of Greece! Further, the Philippians considered themselves to be the fifteenth district of the city of Rome. (Rome had fourteen districts.) Philippians lived in Italy, by their way of thinking. They used Roman coins, built with Roman architecture, and wore the fashions of Rome.

Keep that in mind. Alas, a *Jew* would soon enter Philippi... in fact, not one, but *two* Jews.

Paul arrived in Europe/Greece in autumn, 50.

Gentile church number five was about to be born. But not without a price... a prison cell awaited those two men.

PAUL ENTERS PHILIPPI

Paul arrived in the seaport city of Neapolis* and then walked four miles (10 km) to the city of Philippi.

As soon as the Philippian citizens heard that Claudius had ordered all Jews out of Rome, they simultaneously ordered all Jews out of Philippi and closed the synagogue. That left only *God-fearers* in Philippi. God-fearers were Gentiles who believed in the God of the Jews. By tradition, if a city had no synagogue, they were to meet at the nearest river. The only God-fearers left in Philippi were a lady named Lydia and her friends.

---

* From Troas to Neapolis is 130 nautical miles.

Sometime later, Paul and Silas were arrested and beaten with Roman birch rods (Paul's first Roman beating). They were beaten without a hearing, which was unlawful, as Paul and Silas were citizens of Rome.

The only two Jews in town were two men lying on a cold stone floor, singing. After a dramatic encounter with the city fathers, Paul and Silas received an apology and were begged to leave town.

Paul left Philippi in January of 51. This was the shortest time Paul had ever been in a city and with a church, approximately *three* months.

THE PUZZLEMENT ABOUT LUKE

Suddenly, in the middle of the story as recorded in Acts, Luke begins saying "we." *We who?* Was the "we" Luke? Was it Luke *and* Titus? Had Luke just arrived in Philippi? Had Titus arrived in Philippi? Had Titus been on the second journey from its outset? If so, then had Paul perhaps left Titus in Troas *before* going to Philippi? Had Titus been with Paul in Philippi? When did Luke arrive? And why? And from where?

The answers? We have no idea! We never will.

But this we know: As Paul left Philippi, he asked Luke to remain in Philippi to help a very young church. Paul, Silas, and Timothy went on to the city of Thessalonica.

Paul arrived in Philippi in October, 50.
He departed in January, 51.
Time spent in Philippi—about three months
(See Acts 16:12–40)

WHAT WAS HAPPENING
IN ISRAEL?

The governor of Israel was Cumanus (48–52). The high priest was Ananias, son of Nedebaeus (48–59). Claudius was emperor (41–54) and newly married. Nero was twelve years old. Seneca and Burrus were Nero's teachers and guardians.

Claudius had just given his new wife, Agrippina, the title of *Augusta*, which is the feminine form of Augustus. (She was dreaming of being empress.) Claudius also adopted Nero, thereby making Nero first in line for the throne (by blood and law).

Every Jew on earth was angry with Claudius about the eviction of Jews from Rome.

In all this, the stage was being set for Paul's next letter. The background to I Thessalonians begins 50–51.

THE YEAR 51

ACTS 17:1-20

ROME AND THE EMPIRE

While on their way to the capital of Macedonia, Paul learned that Nero, age thirteen, had received the "Toga Virilis," which meant "the garment of virility." It may well have been Paul's first clear view of the next emperor.

IN ISRAEL

In 51, Governor Ventidius Cumanus (48–52) became embroiled in local problems which eventually resulted in his removal. A group of militant Samaritans attacked a caravan of Galileans on their way to one of the festivals in Jerusalem. A number of people were killed. Governor Cumanus rejected all Jewish pleas for justice. As a result, the indignant Jews living in Galilee hired a brigand by the name of Eleazar ben Dinai to avenge them. His band of thieves attacked the Samaritans. Eleazar proceeded to burn several Samaritan villages, killing all the inhabitants. Cumanus sent his army to arm the Samaritans. The Samaritans, as well as the Roman troops, laid hold of a number of Jews and slew them. It appeared the Samaritans and Roman soldiers were also about to enter Jerusalem. The Romans backed down, but considered this incident to be an act of rebellion. The Jews had taken the matter into their own hands and hired men to carry out their revenge, thereby defying Roman authority.

Once more we see a nation moving restlessly toward armed conflict. In the north, the Syrians always kept a watchful eye on Israel; therefore, the matter between the Samaritans and the Jews was taken to the capital of Syria (Antioch), where the matter was decided in favor of the Jews. At the same time, the high priest had gone to Rome to plead their case. As we shall see, Cumanus was removed from office. All this took place while Paul was on his way to Thessalonica. Did Paul know? Yes, he would have heard of all of this in the marketplace of every town and village he passed through.

Leaving Philippi, Paul moved almost due south toward Thessalonica, which was the capital city of northern Greece (or Macedonia). The population of Thessalonica at that time was approximately twelve thousand people. Paul arrived in Thessalonica in January of 51.*

Paul planted a church in Thessalonica. Later, after he had moved on, he would write the church two letters.

We are able to learn a great deal about the church in Thessalonica from that soon-to-be-written letter. As you will discover, there will be some unique features to this church.

THE THESSALONIAN CHRISTIANS

In Thessalonica there would be violent opposition to the birth of this church. Why? Thessalonica was a "free city." The local officials were in charge without Roman control; however, any hint of disloyalty to Rome would result in the removal of those privileges.

---

* From Philippi to Thessalonica is 98 miles (158 km).

It might well be here that Paul again took thirty-nine lashes,* which Rome allowed the leader of a synagogue to use with no authority from anyone, just as long as it was a Hebrew beating a Hebrew... in a synagogue.

The church's reaction to all this?

It appears they *wanted* to be *persecuted*! It seems that Paul and Silas had told many stories about the church in Jerusalem and the trials which those Christians had passed through. Paul also told how he himself had persecuted the church and how he had later been beaten in Damascus and on Cyprus, as well as being stoned in Lystra *and* being whipped with Roman rods in Philippi. This was a church with an exuberant nature, as well as a great deal of joy. Paul had told them they would also be persecuted and suffer for the faith. Their reaction was *glee*. They could hardly wait.

As it turned out, the city rose to the occasion. The Thessalonian Christians would soon be social outcasts in their own city, disliked by the local government, the leading citizens, *and* the Jewish leaders of the synagogue. In fact, those synagogue leaders were extremely zealous. (These men would soon follow Paul over to the city of Berea. Do we see the possible beginning of a *thorn* now following behind Paul, city after city?)

This we know: Two future church planters were converted to Christ in Thessalonica.

MEET ARISTARCHUS AND SECUNDUS

Early in 51, two young men were brought to Christ. These two men would later become Gentile workers and

---

* This would be Paul's fourth whipping of thirty-nine lashes.

church planters. Their names were Aristarchus and Secundus. Aristarchus would be right in the middle of this entire ongoing saga. In the year 51, we give each man the age of twenty-five. (Aristarchus had only thirteen years left to live.)

One night Paul began talking about the emperor (the *corporate* emperor... Tiberius, Caligula, Claudius). It seems Paul did not like the whole concept of an emperor, which led to...

A STRANGE NIGHT IN THESSALONICA

Sometime during those five months in Thessalonica, Paul began talking about Claudius. (Claudius had expelled the Jews in 49. Many Jews had fled to Greece. Claudius had also recently executed his wife and then married his niece.) Claudius could do all this because there was no law on earth that restrained the emperor from doing anything! The emperor was a man outside of all law... lawless! Paul called the emperor a sinful man under *no* law, a man of lawlessness. Paul also saw the emperor as someone who was opposed to the Jewish messiah.

WHO WAS THE MAN OF SIN?

In the early 1800s, a Bible teacher made a great "to do" of the terms: the man of sin, the man of lawlessness, and the Antichrist. Today virtually everyone is expecting a man of sin and a man of lawlessness to appear, rather than seeing these terms as referring to a man who lived during the first century.* It may be that Paul was simply referring to Claudius.†

---

* This is very definitely the opinion of the author.
† That is, Tiberius, Caligula, Claudius, and later, Nero.

After all, when this futuristic doctrine of a coming man of sin was born, this teacher knew virtually nothing of the history of the Roman Empire during the first century and had no understanding of all those emperors as being perceived as *one* person rather than a series of men. This man's teachings were devoid of totalistic context and historical setting. Beyond that, this teaching (just like Century Twenty-One) had never once read the New Testament in the order it was written. Rather, the New Testament was (and is) read according to the way the books are listed in the Table of Contents, thereby doing what too many do: using a verse here, a verse there, to draw conclusions. That means Paul's letters are read in an order that is nothing less than chaotic. That, in turn, means these men (as we ourselves) arrived at their findings by weaving verses from all over the Scripture and then sewing them together and coming up with some very quaint teachings. "This," they declare, "is what the Bible teaches."

In the light of archaeology, the history of the Roman Empire, the history of Israel, and the experience of Paul of Tarsus, it is far more likely that Paul was referring to the emperor... with good reason. Tiberius, as mentioned before, lived on the island of Capri in private depravity. The emperors who succeeded Tiberius were among some of the most depraved men who ever lived. Paul, a Pharisee, a Jew and a Christian, saw their lives as abhorrent.

THE WORLD UPSIDE DOWN

The Jews from the synagogue had become very zealous. Knowing how sensitive the city fathers were about losing their freedom to the control of the Romans, the Jews accused the Christians of sedition.

The Thessalonian Jewish leaders went even further than just hinting of sedition. They accused Paul and Silas of having caused trouble to the entire inhabited planet.

Where did this statement come from?

Follow with me.

Paul was in Europe...a first. Then Paul was in Philippi... also a first for Paul. No one knew Paul—no one!

Paul then came to Thessalonica and stayed there a maximum of five months. The Thessalonian leaders of the synagogue suddenly said to the people, "Those who have disturbed the entire population of this planet have come here."

Where did that extravagant statement originate? Not in Philippi nor in Thessalonica. Someone told them about Paul in Antioch, Pisidia, Iconium, Lystra, and Derbe. But who was it that told the Thessalonian Jews about what happened in Galatia, which is a long way from Europe *and* Greece *and* Thessalonica?

Could it be that a Jerusalem Jew was now following Paul— even in Greece—just as he had followed him into Galatia? Such men have disturbed many.

LEAVING THESSALONICA

Fearing that the new believers would be accused of treason, Paul left the Thessalonian church.

Paul arrived in Thessalonica in January, 51.
He departed in May, 51.
Time spent in Thessalonica—5 months
(See Acts 17:1–9)

BEREA AND THE NOBLE BEREANS

Paul then crossed a mountain pass (closed in winter) to the city of Berea.* He arrived in Berea in June of 51. The Thessalonian synagogue leaders soon came to Berea. Until their arrival, Paul had made a great deal of progress in Berea. In the synagogue, the Christian Jews were actually being allowed in the room with the Torah. It was read to them every day by the leaders of the synagogue. Unprecedented! (Be assured that the *Gentile* converts were not in that room. It was *Jews* who searched those scrolls.)

Later, when Jewish leaders of the Thessalonian synagogue arrived in Berea, they made serious charges against Paul. With that, the reading of the synagogue scrolls came to an end.

PAUL HAD A "THORN"

Paul never called his thorn an "it." Paul called his thorn a "him." The thorn was a *man*, and his task was to follow Paul everywhere and seek to destroy him, his character, and any church he raised up.

This man told the Thessalonian Jewish leaders of Paul's stormy life from Damascus, Israel, Antioch, and Galatia. In his view, Paul was a man who had disturbed the population of the entire inhabited planet.

Nor would the thorn, which entered Paul's life in 50, relent until Paul was on a prison ship headed to Rome in 61.

---

* From Thessalonica to the resort town of Berea is 45 miles (73 km).

SOPATER

One of the converts in Berea was a young Jew named *Sopater*. We will estimate Sopater to be age twenty-five in the year 51. Sopater would later become one of eight workers who were trained by Paul.

Because of the zeal of the Thessalonian leaders, the situation in Berea became so grim that the brothers and sisters in Berea escorted Paul out of town to a nearby ferry. Silas and Timothy remained in Berea and Thessalonica. After that, Paul came to the fabled city of Athens, one of the most influential cities in all human history. Athens is still called the cradle of Western civilization.

(At this time, the Thessalonian believers were having a marvelous time reveling in their persecution. It appears the Bereans were also faring well.)

Paul arrived in Berea in June, 51.

He departed in September, 51.

Time spent in Berea—4 months

(See Acts 17:10–15)

WORKERS OF THE FUTURE

Add to Titus, Timothy and Gaius, the additional names of Aristarchus, Secundus and Sopater. We now have six men. Paul may have already considered a time in the future when he would train Titus and Timothy and perhaps Gaius. One thing is certain: Train them he will.

ATHENS AND CORINTH

Paul arrived in Athens in November of 51 and departed one month later. At the time Paul was in Athens (Acts

17:16–34), Silas and Timothy were caring for the oppressed churches in Berea and Thessalonica. Later the three met briefly in Athens. Paul sent them back on a brief visit to Philippi and Thessalonica. Paul then headed to the city of Corinth.* He arrived in Corinth in December of 51 (Acts 18:1). Sometime after Paul arrived in Corinth, Timothy and Silas arrived with a large gift for Paul from the church in Philippi.† Having heard a report from Thessalonica, Paul immediately sat down and wrote a letter to the Thessalonians. Paul had been away from Thessalonica for six months.

I Thessalonians was written in Corinth in November, 51 (Acts 18:1).

The background to I Thessalonians had ended. The letter had begun. Who carried the letter up to Thessalonica when Paul finished it? We do not know. What did the letter say?

The church had experienced ostracism from society. Someone in the church died. Paul had not spoken about the Resurrection, so the Thessalonians asked him what happens to Christians after death.

Place this principle right alongside the law of gravity: Know what happened when Paul laid down his pen from writing one letter until the time he picked up his pen to write his next letter, and you will understand each letter.

---

* From Athens to Corinth is 55 miles (8 km).
† It was a large gift indeed. Eleven years later Paul was still thanking Philippi for their gift.

It is now time to stop and read I Thessalonians.* Read it as a story, not searching for verses or theology. When you finish, remember that you will still be in Corinth with Paul, and he will soon write yet another letter. Please note the place in Acts where Paul wrote this letter (Acts 18).

If you have noted what happened in the years 50 and 51, then you read with clarity.

---

* Paul's second letter.

THE YEAR 52

ACTS 18

Paul laid down his pen in November of 51. It was now the year 52. Paul was still a newcomer to Corinth. For the next six months, Paul labored in Corinth as a tentmaker. Now Corinth was running over with Jews who had fled Rome.

Just after arriving in Corinth, Paul wrote to the Thessalonians, and he met Priscilla and Aquila. Aquila was a Jew who had recently fled Rome. He was also a tentmaker. The two men opened a tent making and tent repair business.

Priscilla was a different sort of person. Tradition tells us that Priscilla was royalty, but if she was Jewish, then Roman royalty was impossible. Did Aquila fall in love with Gentile royalty? We do not know, but she is known in the early traditions of the second century, and the exact location of her (future) home in Rome is known as well. Its location was Aventine Hill.

One thing is certain. Priscilla was a bold adventurer. For the sake of the gospel and the church, Priscilla and Aquila moved *three* times in just a period of eight years: from Rome to Corinth in 50; from Corinth to Ephesus in 53; and from Ephesus to Rome in 58. We have here one dear, beloved Christian lady.

IN CORINTH

South of Thessalonica, the city of Corinth, which had always spoken Greek, was urged to switch its primary language to Latin. After all, Corinth was the most multi-tongued city in the world, thanks to the Diolkos on the Isthmus of Corinth, joining the Aegean Sea with the Adriatic Sea. Slaves would use a crane to lift small ships out of the sea. After placing the ship on a large wooden flatbed wagon, slaves (or animals) would pull the ship over a granite road with deeply grooved tracks in which the wheels traveled. At the end of the four-mile journey, the ship and its cargo would be put in the other sea, thereby saving sailors a long and dangerous journey around the Peloponnesian Peninsula.*

* This rail system continued to be used until the year A.D. 883.

The Background to Paul's Third Letter Begins

II Thessalonians

May, 52

Acts 18:1-5

PRINCIPLE:

When Paul lays down his pen from writing a letter, the background to his next letter begins. After four months in Corinth, Paul again sat down to write a letter. Understand what happened in the four months leading up to II Thessalonians and you will understand II Thessalonians.

You do that by:

1. Reading Acts 15:40–18:6, and

2. By inverting, or mirroring, II Thessalonians, which will reveal to you what had happened in Thessalonica during those four months.

Paul's *third* letter, being the second letter to the church in Thessalonica, was penned in April of the year 52. What provoked this letter? What happened in the five months between I Thessalonians and II Thessalonians? After Paul wrote I Thessalonians, some of the very zealous Thessalonians had "overshot the mark." Paul had written about the coming of Christ. Some of them, sure the Lord would come back before breakfast, had quit working. Now these zealous Christians were at times showing up for meals at the homes of those who were still working!

Paul's second letter was an *adjusting* letter. The letter's point can be summed up in one sentence: "He who does not work does not eat." One Bible commentary stated: "Paul was very strong in teaching the Resurrection and the return of Christ while in Thessalonica." The opposite is true. While there, Paul probably never referred to the subject.

It is now time to read Paul's second letter to the ecclesia in Thessalonica.*

---

* Anytime you quote Thessalonians, remember it was written by a church planter to a church. It was *not* written to *any* individual, including you or me.

THE BACKGROUND TO I CORINTHIANS BEGINS HERE

(Paul's Fourth Letter)
52-57

Acts 18:5-19:23

Paul laid down his pen in the year 52. It will be five years before Paul writes letter number four. We shall see the events of those five years, all of which provoked Paul to write I Corinthians. Because there are five years between those letters and because those years explain I Corinthians, we need to be equally aware of those events.

PRINCIPLE:

Know what happened in the years
leading up to the first letter to the Corinthians
and you will understand I Corinthians.

1. Read Luke's account of those five years.

2. Then invert, or mirror, I Corinthians, which is no small task, as it contains five years of events.

Paul had been in Corinth some four months when he wrote II Thessalonians. He was there another fourteen months. This was his longest stay, up until now. Eighteen months is a very short time for leaving a church on its own, especially one so multi-cultural, multi-lingual, and multi-opinionated.

Paul was in Corinth through the year 52 and half of 53.

By then, Paul had two towering goals. The first was new: to train men. After all, Paul realized he could be killed at any moment! The second was to plant the church in Rome... even though *he* could not go to Rome. It was virtually impossible for him to go because of the edict of Claudius banning Jews from Rome.

One day Paul will need Priscilla, on two grand occasions: to start the church in Ephesus, and later the church in Rome.

ROME AND THE EMPIRE

At this time, the emperor appointed Gallio governor of Achaia (southern Greece).

It appears that at this time Claudius was having doubts about the thirteen-year-old Nero's being fit to be the next emperor. His doubts were well founded.

ISRAEL

Cumanus had a major problem. Samaritans had attacked innocent Jews. The action Cumanus took—one of extreme violence against the Samaritans—cost him his governorship.

A man named Felix was his replacement.

Felix was ill-suited for this position.

—Josephus

Felix has taken the place of Cumanus and will rule until the year 60. Paul will meet Felix face to face in the year 58, as his prisoner in the governor's palace until 60.

During a festival in Jerusalem, some Roman soldiers were forced to kill some rioting Jews. Out of the desire for revenge grew a secret society of Jews that had a unique way to assassinate its enemies. During a festival, one of these men would approach a Roman sympathizer and stab him. They would come to be known as the Sicarii...the Daggermen.

We come to the year 53. Paul's next letter would not be written for five years.

After much trouble and a near riot in Corinth, once more Paul left a church he had raised up, making a total of eight churches he had left all on their own.

(There is no mention of elders in either I or II Thessalonians.)

When Paul first strode into the streets of Corinth, his displeasure with the Emperor Claudius must have increased. Corinth was filled with fleeing Jews, as Corinth was one of the nearest major cities outside Rome.

Now, eighteen months later, Paul left that patch-quilt church on his way to yet another city in yet another province. He was on his way to Ephesus for a brief inspection of that city. At his side were Priscilla and Aquila. (Priscilla is twenty-five; Aquila is thirty. We will see them grow old together, to the very end of the entire saga.)

Once more let us look at the record at the end of Paul's second journey.

Paul *arrived* in Corinth . . . . November, 51
Paul *departed* from Corinth . . . . May, 53
   Total time spent in Corinth . . . . . 18 months

BOOK III

THE EPHESIAN LINE
53-70

(The churches which were raised up
by the men Paul trained)

Acts 18:3–28:31

The Gentile churches were raised up "Paul's style." The churches which would come out of the Ephesian line of churches would be raised up by workers whom Paul trained. These men would also begin taking care of the previous churches, the ones in Galatia and Greece.

Actually, these men were *first* trained simply by being in church life and then brought from all over the empire to help found the church in Ephesus. *Then* they were trained further in church life.

This is not the seminary way nor the Bible school way. This was Paul's way, and even the Lord's way, to train men. Here, presented for the first time, is the scriptural way for men to be trained as workers. Note that the traveling church planters and the church are at the heart of it all...with Christ Himself central.

The Background to Paul's Third Church Planting Journey Begins Here

THE YEAR 53

ACTS 18

Paul sailed northeast up the Aegean Sea to the world's most revered city, beautiful Ephesus.*

Priscilla and Aquila disembarked with Paul. Priscilla promptly bought a house!

It was July of 53 (Acts 18:19–20). After being warmly received by the synagogue, Paul turned toward his home in Antioch. It would be a year before Paul would return to Ephesus.

On the way to Antioch, Paul, Silas and Timothy stopped in Jerusalem.† Be careful not to miss this sentence: "Paul then reported to *the church*." "The church" is a reference to the church in Jerusalem, a point often overlooked (July, 53; Acts 18:22). This is now Paul's fourth visit to the church in Jerusalem. By 58, he will be the most hated man in Judea. We can surmise that this change of attitude came about by a copy of the letter to the Galatians circulating in Judea. Was Paul's thorn still at work to destroy him?

Timothy, the half-Jew, toured Jerusalem. What an experience for a young man from an obscure town in Galatia.

There will be one more visit to the church in Jerusalem... his last!

HOME TO ANTIOCH

Paul's second journey ended in Jerusalem. Silas, like Barnabas, did not go on with Paul on the third journey. Can

---

* From Corinth to Ephesus is estimated to be 240 nautical miles.
† From Ephesus to Jerusalem is 616 miles.

you blame him? In fact, no man who had been with Paul on his first journey would have ever dreamed of being with him on his second journey. And anyone who had been with Paul on his second journey would not dream of being with him on a third journey.

Departing Jerusalem, Paul and Timothy walked north toward Antioch,* there to report to his home church (Acts 18:22), arriving in Antioch in the summer of 53.

Paul spent one year in Antioch. Why? He was preparing for journey three.

PAUL'S PREPARATION FOR JOURNEY THREE

Paul had a very clear plan. (In the first two journeys, Paul had none.)

This time Paul was very busy writing letters... letters to Gentile churches, as well as to some special friends and kinsmen. What did his letters say? We feel certain he wrote to the church in Derbe, Galatia: *I am coming for my third visit. When I leave, I will take Gaius with me. From Derbe I will go on to Ephesus. There I will raise up a church, and I will train six men. Gaius is one of these six men.*

After that, Paul wrote a brief note to the churches in Thessalonica and Berea. The essence of that note?

I will be coming through Greece on my way to plant a church in Ephesus, with a special purpose—to aid the churches which exist and to raise up future churches. I will take Aristarchus Secundus, and Sopater with me. I will train these men as workers.

---

* From Jerusalem to Antioch is 300 miles.

Note:

Every one of these six men was coming to Ephesus with one great qualification. Each man had *church life* experience. Each had seen at least one church born *and* knew several nearby churches. All six men would witness the birth of yet another church... the one Paul was about to raise up in Ephesus.

- This is the way the church is *supposed* to be.
- This is the way churches are *supposed* to be raised up.
- This is the way men are *supposed* to be trained for the Lord's work.
- This is the way all churches are *supposed* to be cared for... temporarily... by infrequent visits, by traveling workers, raised up Ephesian style!
- It is now time for Christians of our day to stop supposing and get back to the way it was done in Century One.

Be sure, dear reader, that Paul's way is better than a seminary.

As Paul left Antioch, Timothy of Lystra and Titus of Antioch were at his side. During this year, Priscilla and Aquila were in Ephesus awaiting Paul and his company.

We have seen the churches which came out of Jerusalem. We have seen the unique churches which came out of the church at Antioch. We are about to see a new line of churches or, at least, a totally new way a church is born, and how men were trained as workers, first-century style.

In the meantime, a traveling Jewish-Greek philosopher arrived in Ephesus. Priscilla led him to the Lord and then sent him to Corinth to become a part of the church there. The man's name was Apollos. Rather than sitting down as a new Christian in the church, this Greek orator almost took over the whole church. We will hear more about Apollos later.

THE
THIRD
JOURNEY BEGINS

**Paul visited all of the eight churches at the outset of his *third* journey.
(Acts 18:23–28)**

LET US NOT FORGET

As we begin journey three, remember that Paul has raised up eight churches. Here are their ages:

FROM CHURCH PLANTING JOURNEY ONE
GALATIA

	Year Church Was Born	Age as of the Year 54
Pisidia's Antioch	47	7 years
Iconium	47	7 years
Lystra*	48	6 years
Derbe*	48	6 years

FROM CHURCH PLANTING JOURNEY TWO
GREECE

Philippi	50	4 years
Thessalonica*	51	3 years
Berea*	51	3 years
Corinth	Late 51	3 years

Paul visits every one of these churches en route to Ephesus in the year 54. Paul will *never* see these churches again *after* the year 57. Who took care of them? It was these six men! The torch was passed!!

---

* When Paul stopped at these churches, he picked up Gaius of Derbe, Aristarchus and Secundus of Thessalonica, and Sopater of Berea and took them with him to Ephesus. As to Lystra, Timothy was already with Paul; so was Titus of Antioch. Note how long each man had been in church life.

THE YEAR 54

ACTS 19

ROME AND THE EMPIRE

On October 13 of 54, the Empress Agrippina poisoned her husband Claudius. (Claudius was age 63.) Agrippina saw to it that Nero, her sixteen-year-old son, became the new emperor. Claudius had a son, Britannicus, who was now as good as dead.

Narcissus, who owned a vast international trading company (later mentioned in Romans 16), was later forced to commit suicide, his company seized by the emperor.

At the death of Claudius, Nero made Claudius a god.

Agrippina minted a coin with her own face on it, along with Nero's. (Rome was horrified!) Such was the conversation of every marketplace.

ISRAEL

At this crucial time, we must also know what was happening in Israel in the year 54.

Highwaymen were growing in influence all over Israel. The Sicarii (the Daggermen) were becoming politically powerful. They were eyeing all men who were possible sympathizers of Rome as possible candidates for death.

Governor Felix set out on a determined effort to bring this nation under control. He would fail.

Paul left Antioch on his way to Ephesus with Titus and Timothy at his side. He visited Galatia and picked up Gaius of Derbe. He then sailed to Greece where he picked up Aristarchus and Secundus of Thessalonica and Sopater of Berea. So it was these six men and Paul arrived in Ephesus, summer of 54. (Two more such men will be added while Paul is in Ephesus... Tychicus and Trophimus.)

QUALIFICATIONS FOR BEING TRAINED

The way men are trained is so all-important that we must understand all that went into this one-and-only way in which workers are to be trained.

Let us look at the background of each of these six men as they enter Ephesus.

THE PRE-QUALIFICATIONS OF THE SIX MEN WHO CAME TO EPHESUS TO BE TRAINED

TITUS

- Titus was present when Paul (with Barnabas at his side) arrived at the church in Antioch in 43.
- He was in church life from 43–54, in one of the greatest churches of all time.
- It is stunning to realize that this uncircumcised Gentile was with Paul at the Jerusalem Council. He met the Jerusalem church, the twelve apostles, and the Jerusalem elders. He was present at the debate. He was (est.) age twenty-five that year (50).
- Titus' name was even on the important historic letter signed by all the apostles.

- When Titus returned home to Antioch with Paul, Barnabas, Silas, and Judas (not Iscariot), he also met and spent a great deal of time with John Mark. As you know, Mark later wrote the biography of Jesus. All these men were mentors of Titus.
- The Galatian letter Paul wrote was *almost* certainly delivered to Galatia by Titus.
- There in Galatia, Titus also met Timothy and Gaius.

Dear reader, that is one powerful resume! Titus may, or may not, have been on Paul's second journey. (Luke neglects to mention Titus anywhere in Acts, although Paul refers to Titus often, placing Titus in places where Luke deliberately leaves Titus out.)

Think of how much Titus had to give to those other five men. We might call him the *first* among six cross-pollinators, as each of those men shared their life experiences with the other five.

TIMOTHY

Paul arrived in Lystra, Galatia in the year 48, where one of his converts was Timothy, along with his mother Eunice and his grandmother Lois. Timothy was (est.) eighteen years old in the year 48. Timothy had seen the birth of that church...he was present at the beginning. What more can we say about Timothy?

- Timothy lived in church life in Lystra from 48–50, without Paul or any outside help. He belonged to an *organic* church.

- There in Galatia, Timothy had also visited and seen church life in Pisidia, Iconium, and Derbe.
- Timothy saw a group of religious zealots rip into all of those four churches, saw them attempt to discredit Paul and destroy those churches. *That* is seeing the rich reality of church life. He had stood up to the Judaizers when they came to Galatia...in every church they visited.
- Timothy knew Gaius of Derbe* from 48–50.
- Timothy watched Paul bring the four churches back to grace from the law.
- Silas was Timothy's constant companion for three years—Silas, with all his riches to pass on to Timothy from Silas' experience in Jerusalem.
- Timothy saw Paul raise up the churches in Philippi, Thessalonica, Berea, and Corinth (with all their problems and joys).
- Timothy visited Jerusalem, along with all that must have included.
- Timothy knew Priscilla and Aquila.
- Timothy spent a year with the church in Antioch. If he had not met Titus before then, he spent a year with Titus in Antioch. These two men cross-pollinated their storehouses of incredible experience. Cross-pollination had begun even before Ephesus.
- Timothy and Titus watched Paul make plans for Ephesus.
- Of course, there was the *trip toward* Ephesus, and the reunion with Gaius, Aristarchus, Secundas, and Sopater.

---

* From Lystra to Derbe is 84 miles.

- Timothy saw the great sufferings which a church planter is bound to experience.

GAIUS

- Gaius had his own unique church life experiences. He had been in the church in Derbe from the beginning. He had seen this youngest of all the Galatian churches survive a storm of problems and crises, from 48 all the way through 54, with miniscule help given by Paul.
- Gaius has *that* story to tell Titus, Timothy, and later the other three men. It was a story no one else but Gaius knew! Remember, Galatia is a poor, illiterate land; yet, the youngest, poorest church was the first one attacked by the Pharisees!
- I wish we could know what Gaius knew. We would know what ingredients went into the practical and spiritual survival of the storms of those five years.
- Gaius knew the three other young churches in Galatia. He knew the young, daring Timothy and watched him stand up to the Pharisees in all four churches.
- We estimated Gaius' age as twenty-five in the year 48 and thirty-one in 54, with six years of church life experience. Not a bad resume of a man about to shoulder the work of God!

ARISTARCHUS
SECUNDUS
SOPATER

- We have estimated the age of each of these three men to be twenty-five in the years 51–52. These three men had only *two years* of church life experience before leaving northern Greece (Thessalonica and Berea) and entering Ephesus. Luke called their country, northern Greece, Macedonia, "the upper country." That area was *almost* due east across the Aegean Sea to Ephesus (Acts 19:1).

- These three men had been present from the beginning of the birth of these two churches.
- They watched Silas and Timothy remain in those two cities to help in the violent birth of the churches.
- They saw the Thessalonian church's reaction to persecution (and that church knew *much* persecution). Later, they saw the comedy of errors the church in Thessalonica went through as they became caught up in the hysteria of the possible end of the world.
- These three men also knew what it was like to see a church receive *two* letters from Paul.
- They had also become familiar with the grace and caring the church in Philippi showered on Paul...led by Lydia.

So it is, there were six men who entered Ephesus,* with enough experience to give, in cross-pollination each with the others, to equip any man for any work. To add to that, these men are about to *live with Paul* for three years...and then tour Jerusalem for a graduation present!

---

* There was another young man. His name was Epaphras. He did not appear until the year 63. He raised up three churches on his own. He then traveled to Rome to see Paul, and while there he drew from Paul's church planting experiences. Epaphras is the rare exception that makes the rule.

REALITY CHECK

Do we raise up workers today in the way they were in Century One?

The question supplies its own answer. Seminaries and Bible schools are designed after the Greek model of training men. After two hundred years, have they produced a revolutionist such as Paul, or even someone who knows the New Testament in the order it was originally written? In Century One, training was in the hands of church planters, and it had a pattern to follow. That pattern looked a great deal like the way Jesus trained men. That training, dear reader, was not a Greek-Western way of training men. Both the Lord's way and Paul's way were rooted in bedrock day-to-day reality.

To this pattern, which was given to us by the Lord and by Paul, we *must* return.

We now look closely at what else happened in this unprecedented year of 54.

THE OTHER EVENTS OF THE YEAR 54

ISRAEL

The situation was becoming desperate in Israel. The Sicarii, which had begun in rural Galilee, were not only growing in number, but also growing more daring. No one doing business with Rome, or a Roman sympathizer, was safe. The festivals in Jerusalem were no longer festive, but somber, with people becoming paranoid.

Keep all of this in mind as you see Paul enter Ephesus with his eight men.

While the Sicarii were killing the wealthy Jews in Jerusalem and Judea, they had not yet gone international. At the same time, more Pharisees were being added to the church in Jerusalem. Change was everywhere, all of it moving toward legalism and smoldering hate towards Rome.

More and more it was heard, "If we will but revolt against Rome, the *messiah* will appear and throw off the Roman yoke." There was much pressure from Pharisees in the church to a stricter obedience to the law of Moses.

Rumors automatically made Paul suspect. His work with Gentiles was seen as reprehensible. Nor would we be too wide of the mark if we allowed ourselves to believe that a copy of the Galatian letter had reached Jerusalem. That letter, in the eyes of a Pharisee, was pure heresy! The letter's summation by the Judaizers was distilled into this one sentence: "Paul said, 'The Jews who live outside of Israel do not need to be circumcised.'"

By the year 57, the Sicarii would go international. They would be in Asia Minor looking for Paul.

With all this happening, Paul left Antioch and arrived in Ephesus with six men in the summer of 54. Before he entered the city gate, he had twelve converts. One was named Epaenetus (Acts 19:1–2). Paul and company went to a home that had waited a year to receive him...the home of Aquila.

Paul was in Ephesus for three years, raising up a church and training the eight men who were with him. (He added two while he was in Ephesus.) We know little of what occurred in 55 and 56, but we *can* say the church and the training were historic.

Also in 54 was the murder of Claudius, the rise of the power of the Sicarii, and a new sixteen-year-old emperor named Nero.

Agrippina saw herself as empress, ruling the empire through her son; but she had forgotten that not only did she have the blood of mad Caligula in her, but her son also had the blood of that madman in his veins. Agrippina had only four years left to live.

Two young men of Ephesus joined the training...Tychicus and Trophimus. We estimate both to be twenty-five in the year 54.

We come now to the three-year period when Paul and his trainees were in Ephesus.

THE YEAR 55

ACTS 19

Paul made arrangements with a man named Tyrannus to use Tyrannus' school in the middle of the day during siesta time (from one o'clock to four o'clock).

The church in Ephesus would grow rather large in number from Paul's daily preaching.

In seminaries, you sit in a cubicle and learn theology. At the completion of your course, they give you a piece of parchment and send you out to preach every Sunday. These men lived with their teacher. As you will see, when the training was over, Paul took these eight men with him. Let us see what else we can learn from Ephesus and Paul's training.

ROME AND THE EMPIRE

Britannicus, the biological son of Claudius, died by poison at age fourteen. Agrippina issued a coin with her face imposed on the coin, overlaying her face with that of Nero's, an unprecedented act, and very poorly received. The man Seneca, one of Nero's counselors, convinced Nero to take a mistress. Agrippina opposed the idea. (Agrippina was becoming a nuisance to Nero.)

ISRAEL

Agrippa II, son of Agrippa, was given more responsibilities in supervising Judea. He was in training to one day be governor of Judea. He, like all others, could not control the growing unrest in Israel.

By 55, the Sicarii began considering going international... traveling to other nations to kill.

Rumors about Paul were growing.

It is very possible that at this time Peter was becoming one of the most hated people in Israel. After all, Peter was the man who had baptized Gentiles. It is also possible that Peter, with Barnabas at his side, had visited the church in Corinth. Such a visit would have been in 55 or 56.

We now come to the year 56.

The Gospel of Mark was written *circa* 55 or 56. Keep in mind, though, the events of which Mark wrote had taken place in the years 28–30.

Tradition says that John Mark wrote the Gospel of Mark with Peter. Both men were eyewitnesses to the Crucifixion and the Resurrection. According to the age we estimated Mark to be on the Day of Pentecost, John Mark would now be thirty-two years old. The twenty-four-year-old boy who had gone with Paul and Barnabas on their first church planting journey but had turned back would appear to have grown up.

Please do not think in terms of a wide distribution of the writings of Mark just after completion, or of any other manuscript of this era. Copies of anything were few and phenomenally expensive.

THE YEAR 56

ACTS 19

Paul heard of some needs of the church in north Macedonia. He therefore dispatched Timothy and Erastus to Macedonia (Acts 19:22). Paul decided to remain in Ephesus.

THE EMPIRE

The empire was midway through its *Golden Age* (54–68). Nero would be popular for four years (54–58). He was the toast of the known world, his wickedness and delusion not yet realized. Factually, Seneca and Burrus were overseeing the empire. Nero, age eighteen, was indulging himself. He was also growing very impatient with his conniving, manipulative, dominating mother, Agrippina.

ISRAEL

The Sicarii decided to go international. Their influence was now being felt in surrounding countries. Hellenic Jews were becoming fearful of possible assassination. Their first distant victim would be Paul... if they could find him. Was he in Greece, north or south, or Galatia, Syria, or the area surrounding Ephesus? Finding him might not be easy.

It would appear that Paul's problems in Thessalonica and Berea, and the awful reputation he now had in Judea, as well as the soon-to-be international hunt for Paul, had been aided by the man whom Paul would call his *thorn*. Someone had either been following Paul's travels or had been quite busy contacting various synagogues.

This was also the year of the rise of the Zealots. All over Israel people were hearing, "Do not submit to Rome." "Kill any Jews who are for Rome." "Rebel against Rome and the messiah will come." "Loot the houses of those who have gained wealth by cooperating with Rome. Murder them and set fire to their homes."

Josephus wrote of this time, "The effects of their frenzy were thus felt throughout all Judea." (Josephus referred to the Sicarii and the more recent group, the Zealots.) Because of the spiraling number of assassinations, Jerusalem was a city living in daily fear.

It was during this period of time that an Egyptian Jew rose up, proclaiming he was a prophet. He led a multitude of people to the Mount of Olives, promising that divine help would come to them and that he and his followers would take over the city of Jerusalem and set Israel free from the Romans. The Roman governor Felix stepped in and destroyed the entire movement.

Paul, presently in Ephesus, knew *all* of these things. He came to realize that he was the most hated man in Judea.

The long-reigning high priest of Jerusalem, Ananias, son of Nedebaeus, had some very serious problems with some of the priests in Jerusalem, as he had done a great deal of cooperating with the Romans. Ananias would survive until the year 59. In the year 62 the Sicarii would do the unthinkable. They would assassinate the high priest, Joseph. The reason: He was too fraternal with the Roman occupiers.

In the midst of all this tension in Israel, Paul was into his second year of training men and the second year of the life of the church in Ephesus. His influence on the city's population was *extra* extraordinary.

Paul could not help but wonder if the ban preventing Jews from living in Rome might soon be ignored by young Nero. When would Jews be living in Rome again? The ban had been in place six years. Just in case it was not lifted in his lifetime, Paul had come up with an ingenious plan to plant the church in Rome. It would be a Gentile church, Pauline style, without his being present.

Paul also knew if he died at the hands of assassins, the work would go on... through the men he was training. Churches would come out of the Ephesian line of churches, raised up by third-generation workers, Gentile to the core! Ephesus had begun a new line of workers, raised up by a new breed of worker, soon to do some very innovative church planting. Ephesus was a church that was a place for training workers by an old church planter who knew he would soon be facing certain death.

This was God's way of raising up workers. In the training of men, there was first the *Galilean* way, which was the Jesus way. Now there was the *Ephesian* way, a church with men who were being trained by a church planter to be church planters.

When Paul finished his work in Ephesus, he had two plans: to visit the church in Jerusalem, even if it cost him his life; and to plant the church in Rome by an amazing way!

Once more Paul turned to Priscilla! Paul asked Priscilla to move to Rome... the very next year.*

---

* One of the few things that we know about the early church, as far as being able to point to a specific place and say, "This person lived here at this address," is the exact place of Priscilla's home in Rome. It was known even in the second century.

Here is a question for you to consider.

Paul would write a letter to Christians in Rome. On the last page, Paul called over twenty of these Christians by name. He knew them personally. How could Paul personally know so many people who lived in Rome, so intimately? Paul had never even been in Italy. The answer is simple: Paul knew these people *before* they went to Rome. By the year 56, Paul was already considering not only asking Priscilla to move to Rome, but also many other Christians.

We now approach the year 57. This year will move very fast... so fast it is difficult to keep up with. There are four months in that year which are absolutely packed with travel, tactics, more travel, and three new letters by Paul.

THE YEAR 57

ACTS 19

Part of what made the Ephesian line of churches was Paul sending these young men out to nearby towns to preach the gospel and to raise up churches. It may be that some of the churches listed in Revelation were raised up by Paul's eight men. We need to make note of something else. A gentleman named Philemon will come to believe in Christ while visiting Ephesus, from Colossae. So will another man from Colossae, whose name was Epaphras. Epaphras will one day turn out to be a very remarkable man. He will not only become a church planter, but will also wear the name apostle.

In the meantime, people in Ephesus were burning their books of magic. Even sales of silver statues of the goddess Artemis were way down, putting Ephesus into an economic recession. A major disturbance was brewing.

ISRAEL

In Israel, Felix's efforts to stop the Sicarii continued to fail, adding to the sheer terror that now gripped Israel. That terror moved beyond the borders of Israel. The time had come for the most important event in Israel: The Sicarii had finally set out for Asia Minor to find Paul and kill him.

The Sicarii had a *modus operandi* for killing. Each Daggerman would submit one name of a possible victim. The unfortunate person with the most votes would be the one chosen for assassination. After having made their selection by such means, the Sicarii would then pray for the soul of the man whom they were about to murder. In 57, it was Paul who was prayed for.

At the same time, tension in Caesarea was mounting on another front. The Syro-Greek population of Caesarea-by-the-Sea was pressing the emperor for a decision on who would rule that city, Jew or Syrian? (Caesarea was evenly divided in population, half Jews, half Syrians.) Up until this time, the Jews had always had someone in Rome who favored their way of living. The only person at this moment who was sympathetic toward the Jews was Agrippina, yet she had only one year left to live.

This year, while in Ephesus, Paul wrote a letter to the Corinthian church. It is a long letter that does not lend itself to easy reading. He has not written a letter since 52, some five years before. Keep in mind, the background to I Corinthians literally began the day Paul laid down his pen after writing I Thessalonians.*

---

* Paul wrote I Thessalonians *from* Corinth. Five years later, he wrote a letter *to* Corinth. Unless you read Paul's letters chronologically, this can get very confusing.

THE BACKGROUND

TO

I CORINTHIANS

ENDS

(52-57)

Acts 19:23

FIVE YEARS HAVE PASSED
SINCE THE LAST LETTER

Early in the year 57, Paul wrote his first letter to Corinth. Here is the story.

While Paul was ministering in Ephesus, a Christian who was employed by a worldwide trading company named The House of Chloe had informed Paul of a crisis in the church in Corinth* (I Corinthians 1:11).

It had been five years since Paul had raised up the church in Corinth. A great deal had happened in those years.

SUMMARY

Here is a very brief look at those five years.

In the year 54, while Paul was in northern Greece (Acts 19:1), a recent convert had just arrived in southern Greece at exactly the same time. The man was named Apollos. Apollos was a Jew from the philosophical schools of Alexandria. He was a Greek philosopher/orator to the core. Apollos had come to Corinth and rebuked Jews and Greeks with his compound of Jewish Scripture and Greek philosophy. The Greek Christians in Corinth were jubilant, but Apollos had not been careful how he built on Paul's foundation. As a result, the Greeks in the church in Corinth wanted Apollos to be their man. Another group wanted the signs, wonders,

---

* Was the man who was working for the international company called Chloe someone in Corinth who let Paul know about it? Or did that person perhaps come to visit Ephesus? Or was it the other way around? Did someone from Ephesus go to Corinth and see the situation there and inform Paul? We will never know.

and power of Peter to be the hallmark of the Corinthian church. There was a third group who were "of Paul," and even a snooty group who were only "of Jesus."

What a mess Corinth was!

Beyond that, the Jews were also having some internal problems about lawsuits, vegetarianism, and women speaking at the bema in the town square during town meetings. The church therefore drew up a long list of questions to ask Paul.

Paul was heartbroken over all this dissension.

Therefore, in late spring of 57, Paul wrote I Corinthians (Acts 19:23). Paul, living in Ephesus, wrote a long letter to the multi-divided, highly confused church in Corinth.*

As you see, the letter was not gentle.

---

* Who delivered the letter to Corinth? We do not know, but in the next months, Titus would make two trips to Corinth.

It is now time to read I Corinthians.* Make a note in your New Testament, the place in Acts where Paul wrote the letter (Acts 19:23). It is early summer of 57. I Corinthians was written from Ephesus.

Somewhere around the time of Timothy's coming back from Corinth is the time that Paul wrote I Corinthians.

---

* Note that I Corinthians was written to a church, not to an individual—not to you or to me. Its first application is to a church—a church raised up first-century style.

Spring, 57

Paul dispatched Timothy and Erastus to Macedonia (Spring of 57, Acts 19:22). Paul was planning to go to Macedonia (northern Greece) afterward.

Note that this was the time Paul came up with his plan to send a group of believers to Rome by choosing believers from other churches he had planted and having them go to Rome...but first, having all of them to rendezvous in Philippi.

Do we see a gathering at the home of Lydia, with Priscilla coming to Lydia's home first, and waiting there for Paul and about thirty other sojourners? It was from Lydia's home in Philippi that Priscilla and thirty believers would depart for Rome.

In the meantime, a near riot ensued just as Paul laid down his pen after finishing his first letter to the Corinthians.

A silversmith named Demetrius led a wild protest against the presence of Paul and the believers in Ephesus. By means not fully clear, the men in the city rushed into the 24,000-seat, not-yet-completed amphitheater, shouting praise to the local goddess Artemis (Diana).

Paul knew it was time to leave. The Ephesian training had not come to an end, but the training of the Eight, as being located in Ephesus, was over.

All of these eight men were with Paul in what was...

The Background to II Corinthians and Romans Begins

Paul finished writing I Corinthians in mid-57. When he laid down his pen, the background to II Corinthians ... *and* to Romans ... began.

II Corinthians

Fall, 57   Acts 19:23–20:4

The Letter to the Church in Rome

Winter, 57/58   Acts 20:1–4 and Romans 16

There were only four months between I Corinthians and II Corinthians, and they were among the most packed and complex months of Paul's life. Romans and II Corinthians were both written in that short period of time. Therefore, they share a common background. As you read the background to the two letters, the events frequently overlap. We begin with the early part of the background to Romans, though II Corinthians was written a few months before Romans.

1. Luke gives us virtually no information about the events leading up to II Corinthians, and even less about Romans.

2. Fortunately, the two letters provide us with enough information, so invert (mirror) carefully!

What You Are about to Read Are the Most Crammed Months in Paul's Life!

All you are about to read happened in no more than four months.

Before Paul left Ephesus, he asked Priscilla to sell her home in Ephesus and go to Philippi and wait for his arrival and the arrival of at least thirty other believers who would be converging on Philippi *from all over the empire*...all bound for Rome! Priscilla and Aquila arrived in Philippi first. Then came Paul and the Eight (Acts 20:1–3).

The others—about thirty—began to arrive. (We feel sure, if Lydia's house was the point of rendezvous, then Lydia was the perfect hostess...as long as you did what she told you (Acts 16:15b).

It was time for Priscilla to depart Greece, go to Rome, and buy a house there. She would write a letter back to Philippi telling exactly where her new home was located so the thirty would know how to find her new home.

Priscilla and Aquila cut across Greece (going west) until coming to the port city of Dyrrachium.* There at Dyrrachium they boarded a ferry to Brundusium (Italy).†　From there, the couple set out north for Rome.

Paul's eight men watched this drama and perhaps wondered how Paul could think up such a plan and get so many people to help carry it out.

---

* From Philippi to Dyrrachium is 249 miles (400 km).
† From Dyrrachium to Brundusium is 90 nautical miles.

The reason Paul was in Philippi was to send a pre-packaged church to be born full-grown in Rome. How could he do that if he himself could not go to Rome? He would send seasoned Christians to Rome in his place. Because the thirty had all been in church life, because they had come from so many places, and because they were mostly Gentiles, these thirty pilgrims would fit into Rome perfectly. Rome was Gentile and a melting pot of races and cultures.

Here is God's *fourth* way to plant churches. You might say this "Rome way" of planting churches is the reverse of the Jerusalem way. The Jerusalem way of planting churches was many people going out from one church into other towns to plant a Jerusalem version of the church in many places. Paul's way of planting the church in Rome was many people from many places going to one city to plant a church made up of a variety of expressions.

THIRTY UNIQUE PEOPLE RECEIVED
A LETTER FROM PAUL
ROMANS 16
WRITTEN WINTER OF 57/58

Paul personally knew everyone whom he addressed in his letter to the church in Rome. These believers had come from all over the empire, and Paul rendezvoused with them in Philippi. When the time came for the thirty to follow Priscilla and Aquila to Rome, Paul had walked with them to the ferry at Dyrrachium.*

A study of the names of those people is revealing. Their names identified their rank in society and even where they came from.† Many had the names of slaves. Others were names of *freed* slaves.

Paul had written to every one of these saints and asked them to move to Rome. Once they said yes, he asked them to meet him in Philippi before proceeding to Rome.

A CLOSE LOOK AT THOSE NAMES
IN ROMANS 16

Who were the believers who came to Philippi? First, there were Priscilla and Aquila. They were the first to leave Philippi for Rome.

Who else?

Paul asked Epaenetus of Ephesus to go to Rome. Epaenetus could tell newly-arrived Christians in Rome all

---

* From Philippi to Dyrrachium is 249 miles (400 km).
† This can be done because of the surviving records of the census taken by the Roman Empire.

about the church in Ephesus. After all, he was the first *living stone* in that church.

PAUL KNEW THEM ALL WELL

Andronicus and Junia came from faraway Jerusalem to journey to Rome. These two share everything that happened from the years 30 to 44, including Paul's conversion. They were his blood kin.

Look at the terms Paul used in Romans 16: "My beloved . . . fellow worker . . . the approved one . . . my kinsmen." Paul knew these people!

He gave greetings to the household of a man named Aristobulus, as well as a group of believers who found work in Rome in an international conglomerate called Narcissus. Paul mentioned Tryphaena and Tryphosa (almost certainly twins) and Persis, who had worked hard in the Lord. Then Paul came to Rufus. Rufus left Antioch to be part of the church in Rome. Rufus could tell people about his father's carrying the Lord's cross, of helping found the church in Antioch, and how Paul lived in his home in Antioch. Imagine, Rufus' mother had traveled all the way to Rome with her son. (Rufus' mother's name was a name typical of that era. Her name was Simon's Wife.) Rufus had a brother named Alexander. John Mark knew all four of this family, for he mentioned them in his Gospel. Luke mentioned them in Acts!

FIVE YOUNG MEN

Paul greeted five young men who, as a group, had moved to Rome. One of the most fascinating people Paul mentioned was Nereus *and his sister*. (Either Nereus' sister's name was unpronounceable *or* Paul had forgotten her name!) Olympas seems to have brought a large number of people with him to Rome.

Keep in mind, the eight men whom Paul trained had been there in Philippi with Paul. The Eight had come to know the thirty, there in Lydia's living room. Therefore, when Paul wrote his Roman letter, Timothy and Sopater were anxious to send their love.

When all these people had arrived in Philippi and were ready to go to Rome, Paul and the Eight had walked with them across Greece. When Paul said goodbye to them at Dyrrachium, he mentioned he might try to visit Dalmatia. Paul's last words to them were probably, "As soon as I get back to Philippi, I will write you a nice, long letter. In the letter I will let you know if I went up to Dalmatia." Sure enough, Paul wrote the letter we call Romans, and told them he had made it to Dalmatia (Illyricum) as he had hoped.

THE EIGHT WATCHED!

The Eight were still with Paul as he said goodbye to these Rome-bound believers, then went up to Dalmatia and retraced his steps back to Philippi.

Those four packed months were about to come to an end. But Paul did something which would plunge him into despair. Because Paul was anxious to know how Corinth had received his letter, he sent Titus from Philippi to Corinth to find out the state of the Corinthian church and its feelings about Paul. Titus left for Corinth, but suddenly disappeared.

Paul had crossed Greece, seen Dalmatia, and returned to Philippi and to Lydia's home. He would have written a letter to the newly-arrived pilgrims he had sent to Rome (that is, Paul would have written the book of Romans there in Philippi), "but Satan hindered." What did Paul mean by that statement? He meant that he feared the Daggermen had killed Titus, and he was furthermore concerned about that letter he had written to the church in Corinth. Neither Corinth, the churches in northern Greece, nor the church in Troas knew what had happened to Titus. Paul "despaired of life."

PAUL DESPAIRED OF LIFE?

(We are left to wonder what seven future workers must have thought as they watched their beloved Paul "despair of life.")

Finally, Titus safely reappeared. Paul released his pent-up emotions. Titus also relieved Paul of his other fear: The church in Corinth still loved Paul and saw him as their founder. They would follow him, not Peter, not Apollos.

Paul overflowed with joy.

It was late fall or winter of 57.

II CORINTHIANS

It was at this point Paul wrote his second letter to Corinth and sent Titus back to Corinth to deliver it. The letter was unique. It was passionate and very personal. Had Paul not written that letter, we would have known little of the suffering he had passed through in the twenty years of his life and ministry, his shipwrecks (three, so far),* his beatings (eight so far), his horrendous travel conditions, the lies, rumors, injustices, and his incredible staying power. (The man had *no* "suffering threshold" nor comfort zone.) Nor would we have been able to identify the man who followed behind Paul wherever he traveled, always stirring up opposition. (Paul referred to this man, this thorn, as a *he*, not an *it*!).

Paul finished his action-packed four months and returned to Corinth, the seven men and Luke with him. Paul would be in Corinth three months and would finally write that promised letter to the "new Romans."

Note that "Satan hindered," but Satan had only hindered; he did not stop Paul.

So ends the background to II Corinthians and Romans. There are only about three months between II Corinthians and Romans. Both letters share the same background.

We have learned what happened between I Corinthians and II Corinthians/Romans. Knowing what events happened after Paul wrote I Corinthians and before those two letters which followed, we can understand those two letters. And we have now done so!

---

* Now that you have read II Corinthians, ask virtually any Christian how many times Paul had been shipwrecked. The answer will be: three. This is the result of the static, one-dimensional view we have of Scripture, plus the jumbled way Paul's letters are arranged in your New Testament. The correct answer is *four*. Paul had another shipwreck after writing II Corinthians. II Corinthians ends in the winter of 57. Paul's fourth shipwreck was in November of 62, five years *after* Paul told us he had been shipwrecked three times.

It is now time to read II Corinthians
Written at Acts 20:1–3
To the Corinthians
From Philippi, Greece
Late fall, 57

ANOTHER LOOK AT THE LETTER TO ROME

We now have a little more to add about the writing of Romans. Paul once more entered the familiar gates of Corinth. The Eight and Luke were with him. The Eight watched Paul comfort the church and bring her back to her centrality in Christ. They were with him as he wrote the much-promised and delayed letter to the new, but full-grown, church in Rome. (They were awed at the letter's contents.) They watched his audacity as he asked Phoebe to deliver the letter in the dead of winter.

Review of Those Four Packed Months

Because those short four months were so filled with important events, we will review them.*

Priscilla, Paul, the Eight, and thirty pilgrims came to Philippi. Priscilla was the first to voyage to Rome. She wrote back, explaining how to find her home. Paul, the Eight, and the thirty then walked west to the Greek seaport of Dyrrachium. The thirty went by ferry across the Adriatic Sea to Brundusium, Italy. They then walked to Rome. Paul and the Eight, still in Greece, visited the nearby district of Dalmatia. They then returned once more to Philippi.

Paul sent Titus to Corinth. Titus disappeared. The Sicarii were rumored to be in the area. Paul feared Titus had been killed. Titus finally arrived in Philippi with good news from Corinth. Paul wrote the church in Corinth (fall of 57) and sent the letter to Corinth by way of Titus. Paul then left Philippi, visited the churches in Macedonia, and then went down to Corinth. Soon after Paul arrived in Corinth, he wrote the much-delayed and immortal letter which we call Romans. He then sent Phoebe to Rome with the Roman letter.

---

* Bible scholars have often noted how much happened in Acts 20:1–4 and wondered why Luke condensed it all in four lines. My thought? Luke was busy that day and he condensed!

ROMANS, THE UNIQUE

It is now time to finish the background of Paul's letter to those "new Romans" gathering in Priscilla's living room.

(These "new Romans" were actually from Galatia, Greece, Asia Minor, Syria, *and* Judea.)

Romans is different from any other Paul, or anyone else, has ever written. For one, it may be the longest letter ever written in all antiquity.*

Paul wanted his letter to serve as a document to be heard by all who would later become part of the church. In so doing, Paul wrote, for all of us, the full scope of the Christian life and how to experience church life.

Paul handed his letter to Phoebe, who lived nearby to Corinth.†

The background to Romans ends.

It is early winter of the year 58.

---

* Realizing the agony of writing a letter in that age, this letter may have taken a month to write and then have one or two copies created.

† Cenchrea, Phoebe's hometown, was six miles on the east side of Corinth.

It is now time to read Romans.
(Because it was writen so early in 58, we will
cover the events of 58 after reading Romans.)

Written at Acts 20:3, 4

Early winter of 58

HERE IS A WAY TO READ ROMANS

Just before you read Romans, note that Romans is the
only letter Paul wrote that should have the last chapter read
first!

Chapter 16 is a list of the friends Paul had sent to Rome.

After that, read chapters 1, 2, 3, 9, 10, and 11. These
chapters give us the need of salvation for both Jews and
Greeks. Then read chapters 4, 5, 6, 7, and 8. These are about
the Christian life. Chapters 12–15 list almost every problem
Paul or the Gentile churches ever had in church life. (A true
dose of church life *will* be similar.)*

---

* All Christians who live outside a traditional way of meeting should read those
passages carefully, and any man who dares plant churches and leave them on
their own, Pauline style, may well note the closing advice Paul gave to a church.

THE YEAR 58

ACTS 20-22

After Paul sent his letter to Rome, he had many future plans, but, factually, he had only a few months left to be a free man. Most of his remaining life was spent in prison.

NEXT STOP...JERUSALEM?

Luke and the Eight were about to become tourists! Paul was about to take them to Jerusalem.

There was a sudden change in travel plans.

Enter the Daggermen.

For some time, the Sicarii had been searching for Paul. They had finally arrived in Corinth, just as Paul was about to sail for Jerusalem. Paul faced a simple question: how to keep from being killed.

Why was this man so hated as to have killers coming all the way to Greece to murder him? The answer may be found in the Galatian letter. For a fuller understanding, we must take a moment to see what was happening in Israel.

ISRAEL

Israel was at the boiling point. Had you been there, you might have expected a revolt at any moment. The governor, Felix, was struggling not to lose control of the highways.

Every month a new Jewish prophet rose up. Further, there was common knowledge that Felix was not above accepting bribes, which only added to the Jewish disdain of him. (At some point between the years 58 and 60, the high priest actually bribed Felix into releasing a group of prisoners whom the high priest wanted set free.)

The Sicarii had grown from being a society into being a dominant political party. These Daggermen were openly operating in Galilee, and more recently even in Judea, gaining political influence and power even there, yet at the same time remaining a secret society, killing anyone "they prayed for."

Then there were the tensions in Rome.

ROME, THE EMPIRE, AND MATRICIDE

In Rome, Nero, now twenty years old, had become totally disenchanted with his nagging, domineering mother Agrippina. She had even dared to enter the throne room, telling Nero what she thought he should do. At that, she sealed her doom. Obviously, Agrippina did not remember her own brother (Caligula) who had once sentenced her to death but decided to banish her instead. Nero would not be so kind. The ruthless empress had given birth to an even more ruthless son. Agrippina had less than one year left to live. The murderess was about to be murdered.

With that as your context, we return to Corinth.

LEAVING CORINTH: HOW TO OUTFOX THE ASSASSINS

No Jew was totally safe, not in Galilee and Judea, and now not even in the land of the Gentiles.

And Paul had been "prayed for" by the Sicarii.

The plan of the Christians to save Paul's life? It was to make the Daggermen think Paul was on a ship in the

Corinthian harbor bound for Troas. Instead, the Eight boarded the ship for Troas. (Troas was just across the Aegean Sea.) The Daggermen also got on the ship, expecting to kill Paul while at sea. Paul, accompanied only by Luke, sneaked out of Corinth and walked all the way back to Philippi.

The assassins believed Paul was on that ship bound for Troas. When the ship landed in Troas (in Asia Minor), the men carrying short daggers discovered they had been tricked. They had to leave because devout Jewish pilgrims were headed for Jerusalem to observe the festival of Pentecost.

Also note: The Sicarii had now seen *the Eight*! Especially, it seems, they remembered the face of Trophimus.

The Sicarii and Paul were still on a collision course.

These men were determined to keep a sharp eye for Paul and/or those eight faces. They also knew if they saw any of those eight men in Jerusalem, Paul would be nearby. These Sicarii loathed the thought that at least six *uncircumcised* men were going to tour Jerusalem, with Paul!

Paul and Luke arrived in Philippi in April of 58, where they observed the Passover (Acts 20:1–7).

From Philippi, Paul took a ship to Troas,* where the eight young men were waiting for him. Luke tells us that it took five days to cross the Aegean Sea in order to reach Troas. It should have taken only *two* days. Could it have been bad weather or a fourth shipwreck?

After an unusual visit in Troas (a young man falling out of a window and being resuscitated), Paul made ready to reach Jerusalem, knowing a city of hate was waiting to receive him.

---

* From Philippi to Troas is 130 nautical miles.

Once more Paul placed eight men on a ship without him. This ship was headed to Miletus.* Paul and Luke *walked* from Troas to Miletus.† This was because the Daggermen may have been nearby.

At Miletus, Paul joined his eight fellow sojourners. There in Miletus, Paul faced some hard facts. He had become the most hated man in Israel, yet he was determined to go there. Why? To preserve the now fragile unity between the Gentile churches and the Jewish churches. The best way to do that was to prove to all men that he, Paul, was a totally orthodox Jew. You can be sure the Sicarii and Zealots would not be convinced.

Had copies of Galatians reached Jerusalem? If so, zealous Pharisees had good reason to be grim. Galatians could easily be seen as anti-Moses.

As to the assassins, their eyes were searching the crowds for eight very Gentile-looking men, a doctor, and a frail-looking Jew about sixty years old.

It is hard to believe that a nation such as Israel, teetering on revolt, could hold together another six years. Such was the report Paul gave to the Ephesian elders.

At the time Paul met with the Ephesian elders, the church was four years old (late spring, 58). One of the most moving passages in all the New Testament is found here on the shores of Miletus (Acts 20:17). Today it is used to glorify elders. Paul would later tell Timothy that "all of Asia Minor (primarily Ephesus) have left me." Is it possible that includes these vaunted elders?

* 158 nautical miles.
† From Troas to Miletus is 320 miles.

242

Paul bid the Ephesians a last farewell. (If any of them ever saw Paul again, it might have been when some from Asia Minor visited him in prison in Rome in the year 67.)

Paul was committed to go to Jerusalem. Once more eight men watched the unwavering determination of a man to fulfill his calling. Paul had one mind—to keep the unity between the Jewish and Gentile churches. So it was that Paul left Miletus and journeyed on to Ptolemais* to what appeared to be certain death.

From Ptolemais they sailed thirty-two nautical miles to Caesarea-by-the-Sea. Beside Paul were the Eight and Luke (Acts 21:7-15).

What a "seminary education" these men had!

Those who had tried *once* to kill Paul in Corinth and *twice* in Asia Minor were now waiting and watching for him, dare he enter the *Holy City*!

It was May of 58.

Nero and Paul had ten years left to live. Felix, governor of Israel, had two years left to reign. The high priest in Jerusalem was Ananias, son of Nedebaeus. He also wanted Paul dead, and would do *anything* to see that he died, truth be vanquished.

When Paul arrived in Jerusalem, he met with the church leaders. They explained the terror, tension, and gravity of the situation in the Holy City, including the fact that Paul was blindly hated. Their advice? Paul needed to dramatically show his devotion to the Law and Jewish tradition. So it was that the leaders of the church in Jerusalem offered Paul a

---

* From Miletus to Ptolemais is 606 nautical miles.

possible solution. Paul, with other devout Jews at his side, would take a vow, shave his head, and enter the temple to fulfill the vow.

On the other hand, the intent of the secret society of Daggermen was to do away with Paul. They saw evil where there was none. A city lived in fear.

The story of the attempt on Paul's life is an example of what has happened to men throughout church history: Ethics away. Truth away. Lie. Do anything, but whatever you do, destroy this man in order to protect God.

Here is the story.

Some of these men who had tried to kill Paul in Asia Minor and Corinth looked at one man who entered the temple with Paul. This man looked a great deal like Trophimus, whom they had seen in Corinth and Troas. The men began screaming, "Paul had brought an unclean Gentile into the temple. Paul had profaned the temple."

The city exploded. Jerusalem was doing the one thing which the Roman Empire absolutely forbade. They *rioted*! (All Jerusalem was in confusion.)

Shortly thereafter, Paul found himself being torn at by his assailants.

Enter the Romans. Paul was rescued from the mob. Before he was taken inside to the Mark Anthony Fortress, Paul spoke to the crowd. It served not only as a prison and as barracks for soldiers, but also as a residence for the Roman governor when in town.

THE YEAR 59

ACTS 23-24

While Paul was sitting in his cell in Caesarea, some very stunning news came to him through his prison bars. In Rome, Nero, now twenty-one, had murdered his famous mother.

It came about in this manner: Nero had taken a mistress, thereby riling his mother, Agrippina. Nero had enough! He constructed a very sinkable ship which sank with Agrippina on board. Alas, to the chagrin of Nero, she swam safely ashore. Hearing this, Nero ordered the Praetorian Guard to kill her. When the soldiers broke into her room, she declared, "Strike first my womb, for it bore Nero."

Nero and Paul had nine years left to live.

From that day forward, Nero was more like his uncle— brutal, sadistic, depraved, and on his way to lunacy. Nero added a new flair to this three-generation nightmare of madness: Nero saw himself as a great singer, a great poet, orator, and actor. (He had already made one private performance in Naples.) Lacking the judgment to know he had no talent, Nero began living a triple life as an emperor, brute, and star. Rome began to take note. A buffoon was emerging.

ISRAEL

In Israel, Felix's days were numbered. He *had* to be replaced. Felix would end his reign mostly embroiled with the problem of Paul. In late 59, the high priest Ananias, son of Nedebaeus (48–59), came to the palace in Caesarea with some Jerusalem elders and a famous lawyer named Tertullus to present their charges against Paul (Acts 24:3–8).

Paul was brought in and made his defense (Acts 24:10–22). After the hearing, knowing he would be replaced, Felix decided not to do anything with Paul. The nation he had been given to govern was a nation falling apart.

Felix would soon be replaced by Festus. It is difficult to grasp, but with all the problems the new governor faced, the *greatest* problem was Paul. The Jewish leaders let Festus know what they wanted dealt with *first*: Paul! Paul remained in jail. Luke continued his research. Everywhere it was whispered, "If we will but revolt, the messiah will appear." And every time a Jewish believer heard this, he remembered the words of *his* Messiah: "When the army of the Gentiles approach Jerusalem, flee!"

PAUL ON TRIAL
ACTS 24:1–27

Paul remained a prisoner in Herod's palace* throughout the remainder of the year 58. In the meantime, Felix was seeing his world fall apart. He had essentially lost control of the province. As to Paul, even though Felix had given Paul a hearing twelve days after his arrest, he was trying to postpone making a decision about what to do with Paul. It never occurred to Felix that Paul might ask to be judged by the emperor himself. What Felix *did* know was that if he turned Paul over to the Jewish leaders, they would kill him. If he set Paul free, there would be violent reaction in a world on the brink. Felix stalled. (He had only two more years to rule Israel.)

---

* Herod's Praetorium... the governor's official residence.

From the time of that arrest, Paul would wear chains until he died. For the next three years (58–60), he would be the most infamous prisoner in Israel (Acts 21:27–23:30).

Five days after his arrest, Paul was brought down to the Hall of Polished Stones. Who was in that room? Paul stood before the entire Sanhedrin and the high priest Ananias, as well as Pharisees and Sadducees. Ananias ordered Paul to be slapped.*

Paul was taken back to the Fortress, not as a prisoner, but for safety's sake. While Paul slept, it seems the Lord appeared and stood beside him, saying, "You testified for me well in Jerusalem. You shall also testify for me in Rome."

THE GOSPEL OF MATTHEW WAS WRITTEN

In *circa* 58–60, Matthew finished writing the biography of Jesus Christ. You might call it "Mark-plus." It appears Matthew saw that John Mark's biography had left out a great deal, including the Lord's genealogy. At this point (*circa* 58), Paul had written six letters; the Gospel of Mark had been written; and now Matthew's Gospel had been added. It has been thirty years since Pentecost. Eight books of the New Testament now exist. Nineteen have not yet been written.

LUKE AT WORK IN ISRAEL

What we may not remember is that Paul had his own private physician with him. This physician was also an

---

* It is a year after II Corinthians, but we cannot help ask, "Was Paul's *thorn* still around? Was he in that room?" This author believes he was.

amateur writer. Luke was working on a version of the Lord's life, for Gentiles. In order to collect material for his book, Luke interviewed the apostles, eyewitnesses, *and* Mary, who would have been about age 78–84 by that time. Perhaps Paul the prisoner heard of Matthew's Gospel. For certain, he heard a great deal from Luke about his version. Can we be allowed to wonder if Mary sang for Luke the song which she sang on the day the heavenly messenger announced the conception of her Son?

What happened to the Eight? After all, Paul would be in prison for four years (58–61).

While Luke was writing a *third* biography of Jesus Christ, he was also hearing the stories of the Day of Pentecost and the years following. He would put those stories together. Later, he came up with another inspiration!

While gathering information for the first years of the church, it occurred to Luke to also write a few words on behalf of a dear friend of his, to clear up a great deal of misunderstanding about his friend. Later, probably while in Rome, he would decide to combine the history of the first few years of the church with the history of Paul's ministry in one book. He would call it *The Acts of the Church Planters*. Luke had good reason for writing a defense of Paul. After all, at that moment Paul had the worst reputation of any believer in existence. Most of what was being said about Paul was not true.

While Paul sat in prison in Caesarea and then in Rome, a first-century historian was being born in the beloved physician.

WHERE WERE THE EIGHT?

What happened to the Eight? We do not know, but chances are that Paul scattered them out to churches in Galatia, Greece, Syria, and Asia Minor.*

There are two men who stayed in Caesarea, Aristarchus and Luke. During Paul's imprisonment, Paul will hear about the amazing man from Colossae named Epaphras.

PAUL, MORE INFLUENCE THAN WE IMAGINE

Consider this: Paul wrote the world's first piece of Christian literature, that is, the first piece of the New Testament.

Mark, a friend of his, wrote the first Gospel.

A traveling companion, Luke, wrote a third Gospel.

Paul's dear friend, Luke, wrote Acts, which is *all* we know of the earliest days.

When Paul rebuked Peter, he may have saved us from a Christian faith that would have been Christ *plus* circumcision.

And Paul wrote over half of the entire New Testament!

We now come to the year 60, a year of rumors, murder, intrigue, threats of revolt, and matricide.

---

* Later, Paul called most of them to visit him in Rome, including John Mark.

THE YEARS 60-61

ACTS 25-26

Early in the year 60, after Paul had been in prison for two years, Felix was succeeded by Porcius Festus. When Festus arrived by ship from Rome, he disembarked at Caesarea and went straight to Jerusalem to meet with the Jewish leaders. The one subject was Paul. "We want Paul. We want him brought to Jerusalem. We want him placed on trial *here*." The reason was simple. Once in Jerusalem, they would murder Paul.

In the meantime, Paul was in Caesarea. Festus spent about eight days in Jerusalem on *one* subject—Paul. The new governor promised the Jewish leaders to look into this odd matter. Then he entered Caesarea. Festus invited the high priest and company to Caesarea. They came. Murder was their only intent. The next day, Festus took his seat on the tribunal and ordered Paul to be brought in. Were the Daggermen present? If so, all one had to do was reach for a dagger and lunge toward Paul. A flashing sword to his head would quickly follow. There were no takers that day. Perhaps the *thorn* was also there. We do know Luke was present with his historian's mind in full focus.

At last Paul stood before his Jerusalem enemies. The charges against Paul could not be substantiated. In order to curry favor with the Jews, the new governor asked Paul to appear before him in Jerusalem.

In Paul's mind, a trial in Jerusalem seemed certain death. There was only one way out. Paul could both save his life *and* reach Rome. Paul announced, "As a Roman citizen, I appeal to Caesar." Festus, thrown off guard, consulted his advisors. Festus then announced, "You have appealed to Caesar; to Caesar you shall go."

Paul was finally on his way to Rome. He had even won a free trip there, paid for at government expense. Still, Paul's departure was not immediate.

While Paul was waiting to be sent to Rome, Agrippa II and his sister Bernice came to Caesarea to pay their respects to the new governor. What a sight! Such pomp and ceremony! Luke recorded the entire event, telling the story as an *eyewitness*. Young Agrippa II was given a small area of Galilee (called Abilene) to rule over, with the thought that he might one day rule Israel, as his father once had.

By summer, Festus had arranged for Paul to travel by prison ship to Rome. (There were over two hundred criminals on board, most to be slain at one of the events in the *Circus Maximus* or some other arena.)

Luke would be with Paul on that ship, continuing his eyewitness account. In fact, Luke would record that journey in more detail than any other single event found in the Bible.

Also with Paul was Aristarchus of Thessalonica. (Aristarchus had four years left to live.) There they were: Paul, a medical doctor/historian, and one of the Eight.

Where were the others of the Eight? Either they all waited in Judea during Paul's imprisonment (58–60), which is unlikely, or Paul had sent them out to other parts of the empire to preach the gospel, raise up new churches, leave those churches for a while, and care for the Gentile churches. Those men were all prepared for the task.

ISRAEL

When Felix was replaced in 60, the countryside was almost totally controlled by Brigands. Another Jewish prophet arose that year who led a group of devout Jews who wanted to leave the troubled cities and live in the wilderness. Later, the new governor, Festus, fearing trouble, "cut them down." Agrippa II had been given some control over the city of Jerusalem. He had the walls of his palace raised up higher to allow Roman guards to peer into the temple area. The high priest, Ishmael (59–61), responded by building the walls of the temple even higher. Festus ordered that the extra height of the temple walls be removed. Ishmael challenged the order by Festus, went to Rome, and protested to Nero. Ishmael won his case, but Nero ordered that Ishmael had to remain in Rome as a hostage as long as Festus was governor.

ROME AND THE EMPIRE

Nero was about to make a decision which would eventually start the Jewish war against Rome. The Syrians and the Jews were fighting hard for control of the capital city of Caesarea. Nero decided that the Syrians would have a slight advantage as the ones who would be controlling the city of Caesarea. It was a small action which Nero took, but one which set the stage for all-out war. (Jews and Syrians had equal rights in Caesarea, but the Syrians were more equal than the Jews!)

In the first few years of the 60s, the Jewish historian Josephus wrote:

It was in those years that were kindled the flames of war.

253

SHIPWRECK FOUR WILL
COME SOON

It is still the year 60. Paul stated he had been shipwrecked *three* times by the year 57 (II Corinthians). He is about to board a ship that will trump any shipwreck he has known. Paul, Luke, and Aristarchus board a large prison ship.

PAUL SETS SAIL FOR ROME
60–61
ACTS 27:1–28:31

Luke's record of Paul's time in Caesarea and until he arrives in Rome takes almost two chapters to tell us the details (the other single largest account of one event in all the Bible).

At a place named Fair Havens, near Crete, Paul predicted disaster if the ship's captain continued on the voyage. His words unheeded, the ship was torn to pieces near the island of Malta. Paul would be on Malta for three months (November–January). Luke's record of the voyage covers from August through January (60–61).

A NEW IMPRISONMENT IN
THE LARGEST CITY ON EARTH

In late February of 61, Paul and company left Malta and boarded another ship bound for Rome. The three, along with two hundred other prisoners, arrived at the seaport city of Puteoli, not far from Rome (123 miles, 198 km).

Paul found some believers in Puteoli and stayed with them for seven days before arriving in Rome. Luke said it so briefly, yet so eloquently, "So it was we came to Rome."

Other believers joined them from as far away as *Three Taverns* (33 miles from Rome). In March of 61, Paul arrived in Rome.

Roman law allowed Paul to live by himself in his own rented room. Paul then met the recently returned Jewish leaders of the newly-opened synagogue. (Jews were now being allowed back into Rome.) The rulers of the synagogue had never heard of Paul. They *had* heard of "the sect."

As Acts ends, Paul had successfully planted the church in Rome, a Gentile church, in the world's most Gentile city.

Luke was continuing to work on a biography of the Lord. Or had he finished it? While Paul ministered from morning until evening to all who came to him in his room, Luke was also working on a history of the church, including an eye-opening defense of Paul *the controversial.*

Luke ended Acts by telling us Paul was imprisoned for two years. Two years was the time a Roman citizen must wait in jail once he uttered the words, "I appeal to Caesar." Those two years were mandatory to discourage Roman citizens from casually uttering those four words. For two years many came to hear Paul, preaching the kingdom of God and teaching the Lord Jesus Christ with all openness, unhindered.

Why did Acts end so *abruptly?* We do not know. This we do know: We can no longer draw on Acts for background information. There are seven more letters of the New Testament which Paul will write.

Acts...Luke...we will miss your help. Fortunately, Paul's letters and the history of the empire and Israel will help us reconstruct the events of the last six years of Paul's life.

THE ESTIMATED AGES OF
THE EIGHT MEN
(IN THE YEAR 60)

Titus	35
Timothy	30
Gaius	37
Aristarchus	34
Secundus	34
Sopater	34
Tychicus	31
Trophimus	31
Let us not forget:	
Luke	51
Priscilla	38
Paul	50

We see how informative it can be to know the age of the main people in *The Story*. Even if we are off a few years, we get an important sense of the passing of time and the growing maturity of these men.* Certainly, if Paul was even twenty-nine when Luke called him a young man, he is fifty-three by the year 60. How could one man get into so much trouble in so short a time? Subtracting five years for his hidden years in Tarsus and three years in prison, that means a span of only eighteen years of ministry... of a man who worked for a living... meaning Paul was not "a full-time Christian worker," nor "a part-time worker." Paul was a *spare-time* Christian worker.

May his tribe increase.

---

* Timothy will be thirty-eight when Paul says, "Let no man despise your youth!"

THE YEARS 61-62

ACTS 27-28

THE YEARS PAUL WAS IN PRISON

The Hebrews were losing their control of the very city in which Paul had recently been imprisoned. Festus was faring no better than Felix had.

While Paul sat in Rome, the very center of the empire, he could hear the noise that went on twenty-four hours a day, making it impossible to sleep. He also heard of the rumblings in Israel. He learned a great deal about Nero. Nero was a night brawler who walked the streets with thugs, finding someone whom he could senselessly beat, just for the fun of it. He also learned that Nero drank too much, ate too much, and was becoming more and more arrogant. Nero would soon be free from all the influences of Seneca and Burrus. Paul heard details about how Nero had put his own mother to death.

He learned of an uprising in the British Isles led by a woman warrior named Boudicca. He also learned about the Roman officer who had defeated her and had been brought home to Rome in victory for his brutality.

Ananus, son of Annas, was high priest for one year (62).

In Israel, there was growing hatred between the Greek-Syrians and the Jews in the capital city of Caesarea.

In the meantime, Paul wrote letters to some of the Eight, asking them to come to Rome.

EPAPHRAS

There was something else which Paul learned. The man Epaphras, living in Colossae (Asia Minor) had raised up a church in his own city. At some time when Epaphras had visited Ephesus, Paul had led him to Christ.*

(I consider this man Epaphras to be one of the most remarkable people in the history of the first-century church.)

THE BACKGROUND TO
THE COLOSSIAN LETTER BEGINS IN 62
WRITTEN FROM ROME
ACTS ENDS

Acts ends abruptly at 28:31 (*circa* 62). We leave Acts with regret. Seven letters will be written after Acts 28:31.

All we see of 58 through 62 is the background to Colossians, especially from the time Paul arrived in Rome in 61 until he picked up his pen to write Colossians.

The population of Colossae was about five thousand. There was one other Christian in that small city, named Philemon, whom Paul had led to Christ when Philemon visited Ephesus. (Is it even possible that Philemon had gone to Ephesus to purchase a *slave*?)

While Paul was in prison, he learned that Epaphras had raised up a church in Colossae. The ecclesia there gathered in the home of Philemon. Not content with *one* church, Epaphras preached the gospel in Laodicea† and Hierapolis,‡ and brought into existence a church in those nearby towns.

---

* From Colossae to Ephesus is 110 miles (138 km).
† From Colossae to Laodicea is 8 miles (13 km).
‡ From Colossae to Hieropolis is 13 miles (21 km).

Much had happened to Paul in 61 and 62. The imprisonment, the voyage to Rome, the shipwreck, and now the impending trial before Nero were more than most men would experience in three lifetimes. But even in the safety of imprisonment, things were not dull, not for a moment.

The year 62 was as packed as were the fall and winter of 57/58.

THE YEAR 62

❧ ACTS IS NO LONGER WITH US ❧

ROME AND THE EMPIRE

One of Nero's closest advisors, Burrus (*circa* 62–63), urged Nero not to divorce his wife, Octavia. Shortly thereafter, Burrus was poisoned. This left Seneca as the only restraining influence on Nero. Nero ordered Seneca to retire. Furthermore, Seneca was told to hand over his vast wealth to Nero. Soon Seneca was dead. Nero divorced Octavia. He married his mistress, Poppaea. (On June 9 of the year 62, Nero had Octavia put to death.) It was also in this year that Nero had the only known male descendant of Tiberius murdered. Nero now had two new advisors. One was the evil Tigellinus, the other Poppaea. They rivaled one another with their twisted deeds.

Epaphras was now on his way to Rome. Paul's request to see the emperor would come to fruition in the year 63 (after waiting two years!).

ISRAEL

After the death of Festus and before the arrival of the new governor Albinus (62–64), the high priest Ananias (62) called the Sanhedrin together and had James, the half brother of Jesus, executed. He did this without the consent of Rome. As soon as Albinus arrived, he had Ananias deposed.

The execution of James terrified the Christian Jews of Jerusalem. It is here that we can be sure the Jewish Christians began considering that they might have to flee Israel.

The Sicarii continued their growth in power.

> The Sicarii grew in number and boldness and proceeded to harass every part of the land.
>
> —Josephus

We come now to Colossians and a sacred cow!

BEFORE WE COME TO THE YEAR 63, LET US PAUSE TO KILL YET ANOTHER SACRED COW!

Epaphras was on his way to Rome. Soon Paul would write a letter to the church Epaphras raised up. But let us look closely at the village of Colossae.

There is a *very* sacred cow which men have found in this letter. But, facts will *not* support this sacred teaching. This sacred cow? The fivefold gifts. Colossians, a letter in the New Testament, is the source of the great term: *fivefold gifts*. But, if you care anything for the context of Colossians, your teaching concerning the fivefold gifts, which is derived from Colossians, will fall apart.

Let us take a close, *revealing* look at Colossians. A large part of our modern labels which we place on men come from that letter, the letter which was written in 63. To fully understand our misunderstanding of Colossae, we need to look no further than the village itself. Colossae was a village! It had a population of no more than five thousand. The people made their living raising sheep and goats. The town was small and poor.

Just nine miles away was the touted city of Laodicea. The only problem was that Laodicea was not yet notorious for being wealthy. (Laodicea got its black eye when John wrote Chapter 3 of Revelation.)

Another nine miles from Colossae was the city of Hierapolis. These three towns were triangular to one another. All were small. Two of these towns were poor.

One man founded all three churches. What he managed to do was nothing less than a phenomenon. If you want to pick on Laodicea, then you have to lay that charge at the feet of Epaphras. On the other hand, if you want to praise Colossae *and* to justify the fivefold gifts, then you must also credit Epaphras and the village of Colossae.

COLOSSAE IS TINY. IT IS NOT A COLOSSEUM!

It is here that we see scholars' utter lack of context, not to mention chronology. Let it be said that in this little town of five thousand, with no more than a living room of Christians, all fitting snugly into Philemon's home, we have turned to that letter to justify *evangelists*... the kind we have today; *teachers*... the kind we have today; *prophets*... *if* we have any today; and *pastors*... the kind we have *today*. Modern-day evangelical practices hang on one sentence in a letter to the Colossians. Christians are noted for saying, "Of course there were pastors in the first century." Because there is a word mentioned once in the New Testament, that does not mean what we have today is what they had in Century One.* What an evangelist is today is *not* what an evangelist was in the first century. What is called a prophet today was *not* a prophet in the first century. What a teacher is today is *not* what a teacher was in the first century. Certainly, what we call a pastor today has absolutely nothing to do with a group of people meeting in Philemon's home.

From the Gospels to Revelation, you cannot find the practice of today's pastor, *anywhere*. You may prove today's

---

* The scene is no less than ridiculous. Imagine today's pastors (plural) sitting in Philemon's living room, all doing what today's pastors do.

pastors by the New Testament: You can only do it by contorting the New Testament and by stand-alone verses. You cannot find the pastor in the first-century story. *The Story* outranks all the contortions of Bible verses. *The Story* outranks verses. If you cannot find today's pastor in *The Story*, then the modern-day pastor did not exist in Century One, nor anything remotely similar. Further, the way Paul raised up organic churches makes such a present-day "pastor" impossible. Finally, we know in history exactly who invented today's pastor. It was invented out of thin air by Martin Luther during the Reformation.

FOR HONESTY'S SAKE

Trying to justify today's "five gifts" listed in Colossians does not work. Try putting today's pastors, teachers, evangelists, apostles, and prophets all in Philemon's living room!

With that in mind, let us go to Rome in the year 63. Epaphras, Tychicus, and Trophimus await us.

So do *four* letters of the New Testament, all written in that year.

THE YEAR 63

Epaphras set out on his way to Rome in 63. He had a lot of questions for Paul!*

(Epaphras' native tongue was the same dialect as spoken in Ephesus, which was also the dialect spoken by Tychicus and Trophimus, both of Ephesus.)

Look at Epaphras' route to Rome. The way to get to Rome from Colossae was to walk from Colossae to Ephesus, then sail to Greece, then walk across Greece and catch a ferry to Brundusium, and then walk north to Rome. There is no question, when Epaphras crossed Greece, he stopped at Philippi. This meant visiting the church in Philippi.

THE RUNAWAY

At this point the plot thickened...very thick indeed! Philemon of Colossae had a slave whose name in Greek meant "profitable." In English we call him Onesimus, which is the Greek pronunciation of the word profitable. When Philemon purchased Onesimus, he hoped his choice would turn out to be profitable. It was *not*. The slave whom Philemon called "profitable" turned out to be a thief and a runaway, and a creative one at that. Onesimus was rebellious. He also stole from Philemon. When Epaphras discovered the runaway slave was following him, they had gone too far to turn back. Epaphras decided to take Onesimus to Rome and let Paul figure out what to do with him. After all, Onesimus'

---

* We will give Epaphras the age of thirty at this time.

deed was punishable by death. At best, his face would be mutilated by a branding iron.

When Epaphras left Philippi, the saints there begged him to come back. They sent money to Paul in prison, and they wrote a letter to Paul begging him to send Epaphras back to them for a prolonged stay. In Philippi, Epaphras was called by his Greek name, *Epaphroditus*. As far as the Philippians were concerned, there was no such person as Epaphras, only Epaphroditus.

After leaving Greece, Epaphras made his way to Rome, with Onesimus in tow. Here was this country boy from central Asia Minor, with a runaway slave, wandering the streets of Rome, trying to find the street address where Paul was. (There were no street names in Rome, only directions. In that maze, directions meant little.) When the two men met, Paul read the Philippian letter and stared at Onesimus! He also listened to Epaphras tell his wonderful story of the three churches in Asia Minor. Paul was impressed.

THE MOST CHRIST-CENTERED BOOK EVER WRITTEN

Now nearly thirty years in Christ, Paul sat down and wrote a letter to the young church in Colossae. That letter was the most Christ-centered, Christological letter ever written.

As soon as Paul laid down his pen, he then wrote a *second* letter, a circuit letter, to Colossae, Laodicea, and Hierapolis.* This letter was tragically misnamed Ephesians. Of Paul's thirteen letters, these are the most profound. The first letter

---

* Some 300 years later, the letter was misnamed!

268

was on the subject of *Christ*; the second letter, probably written at the same time, was on the subject of *the church*. Anything else we know concerning the church today pales in significance as we come to an understanding of this unfathomable letter.

This second letter was written to be read in three villages. That letter should be named II Colossians, or "The Letter Written to Colossae, Laodicea, and Hierapolis." This letter was *never* intended for Ephesus. Ephesus had nothing to do with this letter.

Please stop here and read Colossians and Ephesians. Dare you cross out the word *Ephesians* and write in *II Colossians*? Write me if you do!

It is the year 63. So far, Paul has written two letters while in Rome. Paul sent those letters to three small towns in central Asia Minor. Actually, there was a third letter.

Just as Paul finished Colossians and *II Colossians*.* Epaphras became gravely ill, but not before he and Paul dealt with Onesimus. So was born...

A LETTER TO PHILEMON

The letter to Philemon is actually a very humorous letter. We might say that it had been written by *Paul the Hinter*! The letter is filled with *hints*. He almost tells Philemon to forget the money that was stolen—that Philemon owes Paul more than that amounts to. Paul *almost* said that Onesimus was a very profitable person for Paul, even though he was not profitable for Philemon. Onesimus had been caring for Paul's needs. Paul *almost* said, for that reason, Philemon should forgive Onesimus for Paul's sake. Then Paul hinted that Philemon should set Onesimus free! Just in case Philemon failed to get the hints, Paul said, "I will be released from prison soon. I plan to come to visit you. Prepare a bedroom for me." (Dare Philemon kill Onesimus with Paul present in his home?)

Try to imagine Philemon thinking about Paul living in his home with the knowledge that Philemon had Onesimus' head cut off or his face branded!

---

* Ephesians is *not* the correct name of this letter, nor could it ever be. At best, the letter was to three villages.

It is now time to read Philemon.
It should be a stitch!

OTHER EVENTS IN THE YEAR 63

All of these events happened in the year 63.

Paul was close to the time of his hearing before Nero. Epaphras was ready to leave for Philippi with *three* letters. Then Epaphras became very ill. He must have been close to the edge of death.

Timothy was present. So was Onesimus. Titus was almost certainly present. Also, there was Tychicus, one of the Eight. He was from Asia Minor, as was Epaphras. Tychicus could speak Greek and the local dialect of Colossae.

What could Paul do? Epaphras might die.

THE LETTER TO THE PHILIPPIANS

Paul gave the three letters to Tychicus, telling him to deliver the letters to Colossae. Tychicus was also supposed to pass through Philippi. That is exactly what Tychicus did. The Philippians were shocked! When Tychicus arrived in Philippi, everyone wanted to know if Epaphras was coming. Tychicus informed them that Epaphras was at the point of death. A few days later, Tychicus departed. His destination: Colossae.

The Philippians were mortified. They immediately sent a letter to Paul, asking, "Is Epaphras alive?" Unknown to Tychicus or the Philippians, Epaphras had recovered.

Paul received a first-hand report from the Philippians on how the church in Philippi was doing. (There was a problem between two women workers.) Paul sat down and wrote yet another letter, also in the year 63!

Then Paul must have shocked Epaphras with his next statement. (He should shock some theologians today.) Paul called Epaphras Philippi's apostle.

An apostle? That is dispensationally impossible. There are only fourteen apostles!! Tychicus just received stewardship of central Asia Minor. Epaphras had just been assigned Philippi, northern Greece!!

Reread that sentence: Paul called Epaphras an apostle. Why? Because Epaphras *was* one. The only honest answer that we can give is this: One who raises up churches and leaves those churches, and the churches survive, outside of legalism and institutionalism, may be a *sent one*. If he is driven by nothing else but Christ and the church, if he keeps on being a sent one until his last breath, he most likely *is* one.

This we know: Epaphras took the Philippian letter from Paul, went to Philippi, and did what *sent ones* do. In the Philippian letter, Paul dealt with some local problems. Guess who had to resolve those problems in person!

WHY WILL NOT MODERN TRANSLATIONS TRANSLATE THAT WORD PROPERLY?

I know of *no* translator who will translate that word as *apostle*. Translators call Epaphras a *worker*; they call him an *ambassador*; they call him a *representative*; they call him anything except what the Greek says he is.

Epaphras was a *sent one* sent by a *sent one*. Epaphras was an apostle.*

---

* He planted three strong churches, and those churches survived . . . all planted "Paul style."

Read that word and change your theology. There are more than *fourteen* apostles.

If we had men today who had Paul's capacity to suffer and be abused...if we had men of the indomitable fortitude of Paul...if we would raise up churches the way Paul raised them up, with the depth in Christ in which Paul raised them up...today we might not have such a large number of people who call themselves apostles.

Today, many a man has called himself a prophet who is not one. Many a man has called himself a teacher who is not one. Several million have been called pastor...and I will not finish this sentence. Many of us, including myself, have been called evangelists, and yet that would have meant something else in the first century that it does not mean in modern times.

THE LETTER

The letter Paul wrote to Philippi was a love letter. It was his *beloved* church. He vividly recalled, with the fondest memories, being with the church in the year 51. When Paul finished the letter he handed it to Epaphras/Epaphroditus, who was soon on his way to Greece.

It is now time to read Philippians.

THE YEAR 63 CONTINUES

PAUL BROUGHT BEFORE NERO

Sometime in the year 63, Paul stood before Nero. Be sure Nero would spend no more than two or three seconds with Paul, while Paul desperately tried to deliver his testimony. It is unlikely that Paul even spoke.

Sometime in late 63, Paul was released from prison. Paul then did what he did best ... he *left* the young church in Rome.

Somehow, along the way, Nero had heard about Christians. Where? When? Paul said to the Philippians, "All those in Caesar's household greet you." Someone in Caesar's household had been witnessing to Nero.

NERO'S FANTASY

It was in 63 that Nero was dreaming of a new palace, the grandest one in history, surrounded by over a thousand acres of garden. Nero also planned a *colossus*, that is, a statue of himself.* He even dreamed of changing the name of Rome to Nero-opolis! There was one problem: There was no place to build his grand palace, nor its gardens.

ISRAEL

In the year 63, the temple of Herod the Great was finally completed. In just one year some 18,000 workers were laid off, thereby flooding Judea with massive unemployment and causing a financial disaster.

---

* It would be 90 feet or 140 feet high, depending on the historian you are reading.

It was also in this same year that Joshua, son of Damnaeus, was deposed as high priest after only one year. Joshua, son of Gamaliel, became the new high priest.

The Jews appealed to Nero not to allow Gentiles to control Caesarea. (The final decision would be the spark which ignited a holocaust.)

PAUL'S WHEREABOUTS AFTER HIS RELEASE

Where did Paul go, once released from prison? Tradition says he went to Spain, which would actually mean a place called *Near Spain*. One thing is certain: Paul was not in Rome in the year 64, for the year 64 was one of the best-known years in Christian history, and one of the most tragic.

The Background to Titus, I Peter and I Timothy

64-65

Written by Paul, the Place Unknown

To Timothy in Asia Minor? Titus? Peter? Where they were is unknown.

Here we must not only mirror these three letters, but we must understand what was happening in the pivotal year of 65. The Jewish Christians were leaving Israel in a great, massive exodus, knowing the Romans would soon vanquish Israel and many of these refugees would be joining Gentile churches raised by Paul.

THE YEAR 64

Now we come to the sad and horrid year so familiar to all. It was late on the night of July 18, 64 that Rome burned. Christians were blamed, and then later massacred.

The fire started near the Circus Maximus. There were rumors that soldiers were seen setting fires in a number of locations. The fire soon spread north to the valley near Palatine Hill. One thing is certain. Nero blamed the infinitely tiny group of Christians meeting in Priscilla's home. (Priscilla and Aquila were visiting in Ephesus at the time.)

The city burned for five days and nights. Three districts were totally destroyed and seven were partially destroyed. Only four of the fourteen districts were spared. One of those districts spared was Trans-Tiber, where most Christians lived, making them prime suspects.

Nero was twenty-six years old. He was fat, watery-eyed, delusional, and paranoid. He was also losing favor with the people. He had *four* years left to live. So did Paul.

Nero not only blamed the Christians, but had them arrested and then divided into two groups. One group was brought to the Circus Maximus. They had blood-soaked animal skins tied to their bodies. Starved dogs were loosed on them. The other group had their bodies covered with pitch, then dangled from trees in Nero's garden. Carrying a torch, Nero mounted a chariot and drove under them, setting them aflame as he passed by.

If we are to believe early Christian tradition, one of those believers was one of the Eight, even Aristarchus of Thessalonica. Now there were seven.

There is irony here. Paul had written a letter to a little group of Christians meeting in Priscilla's home. In what we called Chapter 8 of Romans, written to those very believers, Paul had earlier penned these words:

Who will separate us from the love of Christ?
Will tribulation,
distress,
persecution,
famine,
nakedness,
peril,
or sword?
No, in all these tribulations we overwhelmingly
conquer through Christ who loved us.
I am convinced that neither death,
nor life,
nor heavenly messengers,
nor principalities,
nor things present,
nor things to come,
nor powers,
nor height,
nor depth,
nor anything created,
shall separate us from the love of God,
which is in Christ Jesus our Lord.

Those words were written in the year 58 to the recently arrived Christians in Rome. Six years later, those words prophetically came true at the Circus Maximus and in Nero's garden.

Just as the church in Jerusalem had ceased to exist on two occasions, now the church in Rome ceased to exist, for a time.

In the year 49, Claudius was seen as hating Jews and opposed to the Jewish messiah. Now it is *Nero* who is seen by Gentile Christians as being against Christians and *their* Messiah. One, anti to the messiah of the unbelieving Jews, and another to the Christians' Messiah.

Always, it is the *emperor*, the *emperor*, the *emperor* who is *anti*!

JERUSALEM

There was a kidnapping in Jerusalem involving the high priest, the Sicarii, the Roman soldiers, and the temple guards. It was settled by a *bribe* given by the high priest to the Roman governor. Even from the beginning, the governor's control of Israel was limited. (Highwaymen, brigands, and the Sicarii now controlled most of Israel, except the largest cities.)

Albinus was relieved of his office and replaced by a man named Florus (64–66). Florus would be Israel's last Roman governor, ever.

There was this observation which measured Florus:

> Florus took seventeen talents of gold from the temple treasury. His forces then plundered the city. Florus then attempted to capture and control the city of Jerusalem.
> —Josephus

We will be forgiven for saying, Israel looked like it was headed for an "Alamo."

> Israel was on the brink of war, and everyone knew it.
> Florus went into Judea expecting to gain personal wealth.
> —Josephus

As late as 64, there were still Jews who were calling for passive resistance against Rome, but their number was dwindling. The high priest was Matthias, son of Theophilus.

CONSTRUCTION OF NERO'S PALACE BEGINS

During *circa* 64–65, Nero laid claim to the burned out center of the city. He actually seized Rome's center as his own, without paying or providing resettlement. It was not wise for Nero to make so many enemies. Many who lost their real estate were senators. Nonetheless, Nero went forward with his plans for a grand palace surrounded by spacious parks and lakes. The palace would cover two acres. The park would cover 125 acres, that is, one third of Rome!

The damage caused by the fire and the building of the palace and parks put a tremendous strain on the entire empire. Politicians, therefore, did what politicians *always* do: they reduced the size and weight of gold and silver coins. The value of the denarius was also lowered.

Poppaea, Nero's wife, gave birth to a girl. The baby died soon thereafter. Not too long after that, Poppaea conceived again. We will discover in the year 65 what happened to Poppaea and her unborn child.

Nero had four years left to live; Poppaea had one year left to live.

The year 65 was the year of years for Jewish Christians living in Judea. It would also be a busy year for two apostles who would be writing letters, one to Jewish Christians, the other to Gentile Christians.

THE YEAR 65

Now we come to another momentous year in Israel and in the empire. Everyone knew war was inevitable.

Where was Paul in the year 65? Was he still in Near Spain or had he left? We do not know. We do know this: Jewish Christians were leaving Israel *en masse*.

The events which were taking place in the year 65 were what provoked Paul to write the letter to Titus and the letter to Timothy. Peter also wrote a letter to the fleeing Jewish believers in the year 65. All three letters dealt with *one* problem. The best way to see what provoked these letters is to read Paul's letter to Titus *first*, then read I Peter, and finally I Timothy. Before that, understand, What *was* happening in Israel in that year?

THE HEBREWS ARE COMING

The main thrust of what Paul said to Titus is simple:

You have raised up a number of churches on the isle of Crete, *but* you have not ordained a single elder! Many churches... no elders. (It was a Gentile neglect, *not* a Jewish one. Jewish churches had elders and had an elder mentality.) Titus, go to Crete immediately. Ordain elders in every city. Do it quickly. This is urgent because fleeing Jewish Christians are coming.

The Jewish Christians fleeing Israel were pouring into the countries earlier populated by Gentile churches. (Here in the letter to Titus, you and I discover that a church was identified by geography, that is, there is *one* church per city.)

PETER AIDS PAUL BY WRITING A LETTER

Now turn to I Peter. In the opening of that letter, Peter actually lists the places where he was sending his letter. Those places were all places where the churches (one per city) were Gentile churches. The point of Peter's letter is: When you arrive in all those Gentile cities and come to each church, submit to those who are already in authority.

Now turn to I Timothy. Alas, Timothy had done no better than Titus. Gentile workers were not focused on elders. Paul's letter instructs Timothy to ordain elders (quickly)! The Jewish Christians are coming!

TIMOTHY DID NOT KNOW WHAT AN ELDER IS?

There is a mystery here. Paul was explaining to Timothy what an elder is. This is *absurd*.

Timothy had already been with Paul for eighteen years! Timothy had helped raise nearly a dozen churches, plus he had met the Jerusalem church. Timothy did not know what an elder was?! Again...impossible! Obviously, this was not information Timothy needed. But Timothy needed a letter from Paul explaining what an elder was, so the *churches* would know what Timothy was doing in selecting elders. One thing was certain: Peter and Paul were making sure those Gentile churches had elders, and that the Jewish Christians were not to try overthrowing these uncircumcised elders.

Paul had raised up Gentile churches which, though unplanned, would become a safe haven for those fleeing Christian Jews.*

THE TRIUMPH OF PAUL'S MINISTRY

The Gentile faith was about to triumph over the more legalistic-inclined Jewish churches. After all, in a very short time there would not be a single ecclesia gathering in all Israel.

Circumstances were causing grace to triumph!

We must pause and thank Simon Peter. It appears that it is Peter who decided to send out his letter and encouraged Paul to send out his. The two letters certainly complement one another.

If the year 64 was bloody, the year 65 was horrific.

---

* By the year 70, most Christian Jews would have few places to go, except to the land of Gentile churches.

Peter wrote these words to believing Jews: *To those who reside as aliens, scattered throughout Pontus, Galatia, Cappadocia, Asia Minor, and Bithynia, who are chosen...* (I Peter 1:1, 2)

Peter had just listed all the places Paul had planted churches, then urged fleeing Jews to submit to the ones who were in authority in those churches.

By the year 65–66 the Christian Jews were not only being received by the Gentile churches, the refugees were fleeing a holocaust in Israel.

Israel was engaged in the worst *civil* war in all human history.

It is now time for you to read Titus, I Peter, and I Timothy.
Also, the background to II Timothy now begins.

Paul wrote II Timothy from Rome while in prison. Where was Timothy located at the time? Timothy would pass through Troas on his way to Rome, before arriving in the winter of 67–68.

When you invert (mirror) II Timothy, you will find an emotional letter, which must have profoundly affected Timothy. Pay attention to the names of those referred to in this letter. You will notice Paul and John Mark had become friends!

ROME AND THE EMPIRE IN 65

Rome, its emperor, and the army knew it was only a matter of time before Israel revolted. However, they may not have realized to what extent the Jewish people were unique to the rest of the empire. Their commitment to *monotheism* was absolute, as was the depth of their hatred toward Rome. Nor did Romans understand the deep seated belief that, "If we will but revolt, the messiah will appear."

Nero's wife, Poppaea, was pregnant again. In a fit of blind rage, Nero stomped his wife and her unborn child to death. It was the year 65. That was but one small window into the mind of Nero.

In this same year, a widespread plot to assassinate Nero was discovered. Nero, already paranoid, now became even more so. In Rome, the year was marked by murder and forced suicides. Even the highly revered Seneca was forced to suicide, his estate seized.

As to Nero's public concerts, those who attended knew they were under penalty of death if they left the room. It could be accurately said, there has been no sane Caesar since Augustus.

The governor of Israel (governor in name only), Florus, was presiding over chaos. The deranged Nero was about to provoke a civil war in Israel, followed by their rebellion against Rome. Nero did it all by one stroke of the pen.

AN UNDERSTANDING

You will remember that the city of Caesarea was vying for administrative control of the city. There were two hundred years of hate between them brewing under the surface. It was those very Syrians whom the Jews had once defeated when they tried to subdue Israel.

The scene was set for massive revenge, on both sides.

THE YEAR 66

Nero had laid out the plans for his palace and the surrounding acreage. Thousands of artisans, soldiers, and slaves were brought into the city. The palace defied description! Even the ceilings were being adorned with precious stones, thereby recreating the sense of the stars in the sky.

Seeing that Israel was sinking into civil war, Florus decided to confiscate the temple treasury for himself. The result of that act was the first clash in the beginning of a civil war, causing riots, protests and bloodshed.

The high priest was Matthias, son of Theophilus, but not for long.

Josephus summed up the reign of the governor in these words: "He constrained us to go to war. We preferred to perish together rather than perish by degrees."

THOUSANDS OF JEWS SLAUGHTERED

Nero actually ignited the rebellion when he finally placed the Syrian Greek faction in *total* control of the city of Caesarea. The moment this happened, the Syrians seized *thousands* of Jews, forced them into the stadium, and there slaughtered them. (The number of Jews slain that day has been estimated between 2,000 and 20,000.)

The war had begun! The year was 66. Jerusalem was named the new capital of Israel. The provisional government abolished all debt and issued a new "freedom coinage."

But...

There were at least *five* Jewish factions vying for control of Israel. The largest were the Sicarii and the Zealots. Then the five groups all declared war on one another!

THE BLOODIEST OF ALL CIVIL WARS

In the next two years (66–67), over half the entire population of Israel was slaughtered, Jew killing Jew.

Every person in Israel had either killed another Jew or had attempted to do so, or had someone attempt to kill him. In the meantime, the Romans were laying out the logistics of a massive invasion of Israel.

During this period, there were no devout Jewish Christians in Israel. *They* had heeded the words of Jesus Christ, "Flee!"

The new high priest, Ananus, son of Ananus, was now the head of the provisional government (66–68). He had three years left to live. He would preside over the civil war.

BUFFOONERY IN GREECE

In September of 66, Nero, along with his new (third) wife, was on his way to participate in the Olympics in Athens, Greece. Nero, sadistic, depraved and delusional, was about to become a buffoon. Nero entered the Olympic Games as a contestant... it just so happened he "won" over 1800 medals! Now we have Nero *the athlete*. The orator, actor, singer and poet had now become an athlete *and* a buffoon.

While in Athens, Nero appointed Vespasian Flavius to deal with the Jewish revolt... despite previously threatening to kill Vespasian for nodding off during one of Nero's endless concerts. Vespasian would soon bring together the second largest army in all the history of Rome. By the end of the year, sixty thousand Roman soldiers would be on the march, passing through town after town in unbroken columns, a true *tour de force* of the power of Rome.

PAUL ARRESTED AGAIN

Paul, free from prison for the last two years, was rearrested and imprisoned in Rome. Paul would once more wait through the obligatory two years before standing before Nero.

As we close this year, we can ask several questions:

Where was Peter when he wrote II Peter? We are not even absolutely certain that II Peter was Peter's *second*. It might have been his first letter. We do not know.

What else had been written by the year 66? We do not know.

Had Barnabas thought about writing Hebrews?* It was certainly an excellent time to do so. Jews needed to preserve their spiritual and historical heritage, and Gentiles needed to be introduced to the Jewish world. That letter to the Hebrews would do both!!

Paul's *twelve* letters, as well as Mark, Matthew, Luke, Acts, and I Peter, were finished. Hebrews and II Timothy would soon appear.

---

* There is a great deal of theological conjecture over who wrote the letter to the Hebrews, but second-century Christians did not equivocate. They stated that Barnabas had written it. We will, therefore, accept their judgment.

THE YEAR 67

We come now to a year of chaos, sprinkled with insanity.

What was happening in Israel could only be described as a self-inflicted holocaust, a study in massive national suicide. The people in Israel were killing one another in slow motion. It is estimated that half the Jews in Israel killed one another. Then, in Alexandria and throughout Syria, Jews were being attacked and killed. *This* was the *real* tribulation.

The Zealots seized control of the city of Jerusalem. The Sicarii seized the temple. Everyone was looking for the appearance of their messiah.

By land and by sea, Vespasian's army began closing in on Israel. Young Titus Flavius joined his father Vespasian in Israel. He soon took command of one of the Roman legions. (We are also told that Titus Flavius fell in love with Beatrice, the sister of Agrippa II.)

It was also in this year that some of the Sicarii took possession of a mountain fortress built by Herod the Great, called Masada.

The emperor was, in turn, winning the decathlon!

Most of Israel was conquered by the end of the year 67. Jerusalem was surrounded. A classical Roman siege had begun.

Nero, while in Greece, had three senators in Rome executed.

PAUL AND NERO

We must now take a look at Nero and Paul, as the curtain closes on both of their lives. Nero in Greece, Paul in prison.

Unbelievably (!), Nero won every athletic contest. Just as unbelievable, the Greeks then decided to have *all* the Grecian games to be played in Athens in one year, rather than over a four-year period. Greek leaders did this so their athletic emperor could participate in *all* the Greek sports.

While Nero was waiting for the athletes to arrive in Athens, the emperor traveled down to Corinth to open the Isthmian Games. On November 21, Nero declared that Greece would no longer need to pay taxes to Rome. Without realizing it, Nero had signed his own death warrant! Back in Rome, the senate was enraged.

There in Corinth, Nero announced the building of a canal *across* the *Isthmus of Corinth*, thereby joining the Aegean Sea and the Adriatic Sea. Using a solid gold shovel, Nero lifted the first load of dirt to be removed for the canal. Nero then returned to Athens, where he entered every game ever played in Greece... all in a few weeks.

Paul, in prison, was virtually assured he would be sentenced to death.

The rumors of the goings on of Nero in Greece filled the empire. Nero was making a colossal fool of himself.

We now come to...

THE BACKGROUND TO
II TIMOTHY

The background to II Timothy began when Paul was rearrested in the year 66 or 67, and just before Paul was scheduled for his second hearing, the one to decide his fate.

II TIMOTHY

Paul sent a letter to Timothy, asking him to come to Rome before the winter of 68. We have no idea where Timothy was . . . probably in the Asia Minor area. Paul also asked for a cloak, parchment, *and* John Mark! (May we be allowed to believe that Paul was asking John Mark to come to Rome to aid in translating the Gospel of Mark out of Greek into Latin?) This second letter to Timothy was probably sent out in late summer or early fall of the year 67, and written from prison.

We now come to the death of the best-known man in the history of Rome, Italy and the death of the best-known man in the history of Tarsus, Cilicia.

It is now time to read II Timothy... the last of Paul's thirteen letters.

THE YEAR 68

Nero returned to Rome, having won over eighteen hundred contests. It appears that Nero actually believed he had won the athletic contests honestly. When Nero returned to Rome, he found his palace finished. He is quoted as saying, "Finally, a place decent enough for a human to live in!" He would spend very few nights in his new home, now named The Golden House. Soon thereafter, the senate voted Nero to be an enemy of the state. A few days later, Nero, with the assistance of a servant, committed suicide, stabbed in the neck. Nero's final words were, "Oh, what an artist in me dies."

If you are wondering where Nero's palace is located, along with its lakes and gardens, the exact place is quite easy to locate.*

NERO'S PALACE, WHERE?

Receiving an execution reserved only for a Roman citizen, the swiftness of the sword, Paul was beheaded sometime in 68.

Paul is our hero. Nonetheless, even Christians today would most likely have a difficult time with Paul. Paul was in endless trouble, disliked by government, local citizens, and religionists. Dare any man live his kind of life again? He

---

* When Vespasian became emperor, all of the gardens, the statue, and most of the palace were destroyed. Using 20,000 captive Jewish slaves, Vespasian had a stadium built where Nero's palace had stood. Today, that stadium is called the Coliseum. There are a few remains of the palace recently excavated and refurbished.

would be the prize topic and target of men today, especially on the *Internet*.

Few men have ever been made of the material which allows them to live such a life, or endure so much rejection, suffering, and endless innuendos.

We thank God that Luke wrote Paul's biography (Acts 9–28), thereby *somewhat* balancing the *real* truth over against the worldwide *invented* story.

By the year 68, Vespasian's army was at the gates of Jerusalem. At that moment Vespasian heard of Nero's death. He also knew he had the largest army on earth, the best possible qualification for being an emperor. Vespasian turned part of his army over to his son, Titus. Vespasian, with the rest of his vast army, began a long, leisurely journey back to Rome. When Vespasian and his army neared Rome, the senate declared Vespasian to be the next emperor.

Our journey through the first century is coming to an end. So is the story of the practice of first-century Christianity. . . a practice which looks nothing like the practice of Christianity today.

Perhaps there is also a crisis brewing here, at this point. It has to do with you, the reader.

You are not only discovering how much there is to discover about God's Word when Paul's letters are in their proper order, but you also discover the emergence of *The Story* and the first-century *model*.

It is the year 68. What about the Eight, and others?

THE ESTIMATED AGES OF THE EIGHT MEN ON THE DAY PAUL DIED (WINTER OF 68)

Titus	43
Timothy	48*
Gaius	45
Aristarchus	41†
Secundus	41
Sopater	41
Tychicus	39
Trophimus	39
Luke	59

Let us not forget:

Priscilla	46
Epaphras	35
Paul	58

---

* Timothy was thirty-five years old when Paul said to him, "Let no one despise your youth."
† Aristarchus died in the year 64.

THE AGES OF THE CHURCHES
ON THE DAY PAUL DIED
(WINTER OF 68)

GALATIAN CHURCHES	AGE
Pisidia's Antioch	21 years
Iconium	21 years
Lystra	20 years
Derbe	20 years

GREEK CHURCHES	
Philippi	17 years
Thessalonica	17 years
Berea	17 years
Corinth	16 years

ASIA MINOR CHURCHES*	
Ephesus	14 years
Troas	14 years

ONE ITALIAN CHURCH!	
Rome	10 years

---

* Later Asia Minor was to be literally filled with churches.

THE YEAR 69

In July of 69, a cheering Rome found it had a new emperor. On December 1 of 69, the senate officially declared Vespasian to be emperor. Modestly, Vespasian took the throne in January of 70. His son, Titus Flavius, was now in line to be the next emperor after Vespasian.

What happened in the Christian world in the year 69? The pages are blank. They would remain virtually blank until the year 100. Even then, little is known until the year 120.

In the year 69, we have twenty-one of the twenty-seven books of the New Testament in existence, nearly half only recently written.* There would be six more, but we have no idea when those six were written.

---

* Mark, Matthew, Luke, John, Acts, Paul's thirteen letters, I Peter, II Peter, and Hebrews.

THE YEAR 70

We come to that year in which history can tell us of Christians in Century One.

In that year, Titus Flavius received a rumor that the besieged people in Jerusalem had taken to cannibalism. He ended the siege with a massive assault on the temple. (The city had fallen in 69.) Once the Romans entered the temple, no lives were spared. Still, even to the very last moment, Jewish inhabitants were expecting their messiah to appear.

The temple fell to Titus Flavius in August of the year 70. Except for two towers of the wall, the city was destroyed.*

Some twenty thousand Jewish men from all over Israel were later enslaved and taken to Rome to build the *Coliseum* (70–78).

So ends the forty years which shook the world. But what of those six other letters of the New Testament?

---

* Jerusalem was not plowed under until the year 130. Where the temple once stood, a statue of Apollo was erected.

THE REMAINING SIX LETTERS:
WHERE AND WHEN?

HEBREWS

There are twenty-two books of the New Testament that have information about history in them. That history lets us know so much—dates, places, circumstances, and context. The other five letters give *no* context whatsoever. When and where those five letters were written is unknown.

Scholars tend to agree on one point: All were written near or during the time of Nero's persecution and the persecution led by Vespasian's youngest son, Titus Flavius. This would place those writings between 64–68, or around the year 90. Or... *some* may have been written between 64–68, and *some* around the year 90. Only Hebrews gives a one-sentence hint that it may have been written around 68–70: "Timothy has been released from prison" (Hebrews 13:23).

Was Hebrews written by Barnabas? Was it written between 68–70? Where was it written? We do not know. We do know that second-century Christians were confident: They said it was written by Barnabas.

JAMES

James gives us no hint as to when or where it was written. James could have been written as early as the year 40 and as late as 65, either by James, the brother of John, or James, the half-brother of Jesus.

JUDE

We have no idea when Jude was written. It was probably written just before or just after the destruction of Jerusalem. That is a scholarly guess. Any guess to date and time breaks down under scrutiny!

I, II, AND III JOHN

The three letters by John were written by John the Apostle. Were they written after John moved from Israel to Ephesus? The letters are generally assumed to have been written to churches in Asia Minor. There are two estimated dates. The dating is done more from a viewpoint of "last days" theology, rather than by actual evidence of a date. One date is that I John was written somewhere between 65 and 70. The other date is usually set around the year 90.

As to John's reference to the *anti-messiah*, we must face the fact there were not only emperors, but in the minds of the ordinary people in the empire, there was but one emperor—an ageless, dateless persona dating from Caligula through Domitian. This one emperor persecuted Jews because of their messiah in the year 49, and then the Christians' Messiah in 64–68 and in circa 90. The emperor was the anti-messiah. He was many men rolled into one person, and that corporate, ageless, ever-present emperor was *the Antichrist* for both the unbelieving Jews (49) and the Christians (64–90).

Some British teachers of the 1800s, who knew little of context and only stitched together verses and mathematical leaps of logic, were in error about their understanding of the passage in I John!

REVELATION

To say that the letter Revelation is mysterious and enigmatic is to give new meaning to those words.

According to your view of eschatology, this letter was either written in *circa* 68 or around the year 90. If you choose the earlier date, that would mean John wrote this letter while Nero was alive, and that Nero himself is mentioned in this book, or that it was written not long after Nero's death when rumor had it that Nero was *not* dead or had come back to life. That makes Revelation a book of comfort for Christians during the reign of Nero and could be understood by those who first read the book.

The other view, more widely accepted, is that the book was written somewhere around the year 90, during the horrific persecution under Domitian. (In either of these two dates, John was alive, living on the Isle of Patmos.) That later date would place the writing of Revelation during the persecution of Christians (*circa* 85–90), who understood the letter when they read it. The other view, as to the understandability, is that God intended this to be a closed letter until about 1840! As bizarre as that idea is, it is the most widely accepted interpretation of Revelation . . . despite the fact that few realize that what they are taught about Revelation is predicated upon its being a closed book *until* a certain man opened it in the 1800s.

Take your choice.

THE PURPOSE OF THIS BOOK

This book was written for one purpose: for you to compare the present-day practice of our faith as over against the practice of the Christians of the first century.

Most of today's church practices originated around the time of Constantine (300–337) and around the time of the Reformation (1520–1670). That is, the origin of what we are doing today is not based on the New Testament, but the practices we have were picked up along the way in the random meandering of the church's march through church history.*

The question is very simple. Do we continue practicing what we have today, forever making it *look like* it is all very scriptural, Bible-based, and very first-century? Or do we seek a full discovery of Century One and pursue it with all our hearts! Example: the return of the itinerant church planter and the return of the organic nature of the church.

This book, then, boils down to this: It is written for those who have a heart to return to the practices and the *spiritual depths* that were known and experienced in those forty years which shook the world.

Just to be clear, the last thing on earth this author wants to see is someone walk in and say, "Let's have an organic church. Now, turn to chapter... and see what an organic church will look like." Rather, let a man walk into a room of Christians and declare, "I want to show you how to drown in

---

* Yes, after we establish our traditions, we then justify them as scriptural, by contorting *verses*. That is not honest. Accepted, yes... but truly scriptural, no!

the experience of encountering the Lord Jesus Christ. I will do this for six months, with a little practical advice thrown in. Then I will leave you for one or two years."

What a day that will be!

Dear reader, I ask you to join me in reading the New Testament in the order it was written... from henceforth and forevermore.

Want to join in this crusade?

Notice, there is no address here.

If you *do* wish to get in the arena,
you will find a way to contact those
who are pursuing this path.

In fact, nothing created will stop you.

HELPS

READ YOUR NEW TESTAMENT THIS WAY

ACTS 1–13:1

GALATIANS   WRITTEN
  Background begins at Acts 13:1   Summer, 50
  Written at Acts 15:40

I THESSALONIANS
  Background begins at Acts 15:40–18:1   November, 51
  Written at Acts 18:1

II THESSALONIANS
  Background begins Acts 18:1–5   April, 52
  Written at Acts 18:5

I CORINTHIANS
  Background begins at Acts 18:5–19:23   Summer, 57
  Written at Acts 19:23

II CORINTHIANS
  Background begins at Acts 19:23–20:4   Fall, 57
  Written at Acts 20:1–4

ROMANS
  Background begins at Acts 20:1–4   Winter, 57/58
    (plus Romans 16)
  The end of Acts 28:31

COLOSSIANS   63

EPHESIANS   63

PHILEMON   63

Locating the Six Places in Acts Where Paul Wrote His First Letters

You will have three notes to make in your New Testament until Acts ends. Then you will have only one.

WHERE IN ACTS:

GALATIANS:
ACTS 15:40
- The *background* to Galatians begins at Acts 13:1.
- Galatians was written in *late spring of 50*.
- One and one-half years passed before Paul wrote...

I THESSALONIANS:
ACTS 18:1
- The *background* to I Thessalonians begins at Acts 15:40–18:1.
- I Thessalonians was written in *November of 51*.
- Four months passed before Paul wrote...

II THESSALONIANS:
ACTS 18:5
- The *background* to II Thessalonians begins at Acts 18:1–5.
- II Thessalonians was written in *April of 52*.
- Five years passed before Paul wrote...

I CORINTHIANS:
ACTS 19:23
- The *background* to I Corinthians begins at Acts 18:5–19:23.

- I Corinthians was written in *late spring of 57*.
- It was about four very packed months before Paul wrote...

II CORINTHIANS:
ACTS 20:1-3
- The *background* to II Corinthians begins at Acts 19:23–20:4.
- II Corinthians was written in the *fall of 57*.
- Only about one to three months passed before Paul wrote...

ROMANS:
ACTS 20:3, 4
- The *background* to Romans begins at Acts 20:1–4 and in Romans 16. These people in Romans 16 are the ones Paul sent to Rome to rendezvous at Priscilla's home in Rome in autumn/early fall of 57.
- Paul then wrote Romans in *winter of 57/58*.

THE END OF ACTS
28:31

It was five years before Paul wrote another letter. By that time, the history book of Acts had ended (62).

TIME BETWEEN LETTERS

Galatians to I Thessalonians	1 1/2 years (50–51)
I Thessalonians to II Thessalonians	4 months (52)
II Thessalonians to I Corinthians	5 years (52–57)
I Corinthians to II Corinthians	4 months (57)

II Corinthians to Romans	Less than 4 months (57–58)
Romans to Colossians, Ephesians, Philemon, & Philippians	5 years (63)
Colossians to Titus & I Timothy	2 years (65)
Titus and I Timothy to II Timothy	2 years (65–67)

Learn what happened between each letter and you will buffalo Bible scholars.

THIS IS WHERE THE LETTERS WERE WRITTEN

Letter	Reference	Date	Written From/ Sent To
Galatians	Acts 15:40	Late spring, 50	Antioch to Galatia
I Thessalonians	Acts 18:1	November, 51	Southern Greece to Northern Greece
II Thessalonians	Acts 18:5	April, 52	Southern Greece to Northern Greece
I Corinthians	Acts 19:23	Late spring, 57	Ephesus to Corinth
II Corinthians	Acts 20:1–3	Fall, 57	Philippi to Corinth
Romans	Acts 20:3–4	Winter, 57/58	Corinth to Rome

Keep in mind that Acts ended in the year 62. From the years 50–62 only six of Paul's letters were written. The only other books of the New Testament written before the year 62 were probably Mark or Matthew. Most books were written after Acts closes. That is, most were written between the years 63–70.

AFTER ACTS ENDS

You now have only two notations for your margin: 1) the year of the beginning of the background to the letter and 2) the year the letter was written.

LETTER	DATE	WRITTEN FROM/ SENT TO
Colossians	63	Rome to Colossae
Ephesians	63	Rome to Colossae
Philemon	63	Rome to Colossae
Philippians	63	Rome to Philippi
Titus	65	Rome to Crete (?)
I Timothy	65	Rome to Asia Minor
I Peter	65	Peter to fleeing Jews
II Timothy	67*	Rome to Neapolis

---

* The dates of all the other epistles are unknown. Hebrews (68?) II Peter (66?) James, I, II, III John, Jude, Revelation (68 or 90?)

TWELVE NEW HELPS AVAILABLE TO US ONLY WHEN WE HAVE A CHRONOLOGICAL NEW TESTAMENT

You have been introduced to very meaningful aids which can be added only if you move forward, chronologically. As you continue to read your New Testament chronologically for a long period of time, you will naturally discover, on your own, other ways to add to, and build on, a multi-dimensional Bible study.

The simple matter of times, dates, and places often give way to other discoveries which leap out at you.

1. DATING THE WRITING OF PAUL'S LETTERS

We have arranged the letters of Paul in order by the dates he wrote them. From the context we have given, you discover what events happened in any given year in Paul's life, in Rome, in the empire, in Israel, or in the churches to which he wrote.

2. PROPER ORDER OF PAUL'S LETTERS

Galatians; I Thessalonians; II Thessalonians; I Corinthians; II Corinthians; Romans; Colossians; Ephesians; Philemon; Philippians; I Timothy; Titus; II Timothy (all written between the years 50 and 67).

3. TIME BETWEEN PAUL'S LETTERS

There is time which passes between each of Paul's letters. Learn what happened *between* Paul's letters, and a new dimension of understanding is yours. Knowing the events between Paul's letters is crucial, even central. Note the length of time between each letter. That *next* letter becomes crystal clear. Each letter is predicated upon what happened *before* the letter was written. Those events provoked that letter. Note the events and understand the letter.

4. THE LETTER'S BACKGROUND

The *background* to the letter, preceding the writing of the letter.

Illustration: The background to the writing of the Galatian letter began in spring of 47, at Acts 13:1. The background to Galatians continued until spring of 50, to be noted at Acts 15:40.

5. WHERE THE LETTER WAS WRITTEN AND WHERE IT WAS SENT

The *from where/to where* is important. The letter may have been written in one city and sent to another.

Illustration: Galatians was written in spring of 50, from Antioch, Syria. It was sent to four churches in Galatia, central Asia Minor.

6. THE EIGHT

There is a list of the men Paul trained.* All these men already appeared, in their order, before Luke names them. It is all built into the story. The *how*, the *when*, the *where* all become so clear. With Paul's letters in their proper order, these people emerge in full dimension.

---

* See page 313.

7. HOW, WHERE, WHEN, AND WHO?

Pay close attention to the *how, where, when,* and *who* of these men, and the dates of each man's church experience. What happened to each man when Paul raised up a church? What happened to the man when Paul left? This is powerful information, as well as downright shocking!

8. FESTIVALS AND SEASONS

Festivals and seasons, including the month, the week, the day, and, on occasion, even the exact *hour*. A view of our journey through the first century begins to rise out of the ashes of a one-dimensional view, to the first century in three-dimension.

9. MILES

The distance of *miles* between cities and the days needed to travel from one city to another brings us to the reality of first-century travel. It was slow!

10. AGE OF PEOPLE

Giving an age to each person. This, of course, has been a truly new dimension. Forgive us for *our* estimates. Use your own. Nonetheless, estimating the age of each person is an eye opener. Watching a person age over a period of forty years gives us yet another insight into what has previously been a flat-earth view of Scripture. We presently have a New Testament which has no times, no places, no context, no surrounding culture, people, topography, miles, weather, seasons, etc. That same New Testament is cast in an order which gives new meaning to such words as chaos, bizarre, confusing, jumbled, and indecipherable. Such chaos is an invitation to a "verse-istic" captivity and rampant "crossword puzzling" that stupefies the mind. As a result, this leaves that waitress at the truck stop helplessly cut off from understanding—or even reading—the Word of God!

11. SOCIAL, POLITICAL, CULTURAL, SURROUNDINGS

Weather, population, culture, geography, understanding the military, topography, and politics all provide us further help, perhaps—at last—delivering us from our view of the church as formality-driven and static. We have believed that restoring methods was all we needed, utterly overlooking the need of the daily spiritual encounter.

12. CORRELATING ACTS CHAPTERS WITH YEARS

Then, of course, there is the matter of seeing the chapter-year correlation that has been the highway this book has driven on as we journey through the first century.

We *can* know the Scripture far better than we have in centuries past.

THE MOST IMPORTANT OF ALL THESE

It is knowing what happened between Paul's letters which is the key to knowing so much of what has been left out for the last 1800 years.

We need a book that explores all the events which happened before and between Paul's letters.

THE TRIUMPH OF *THE STORY* OVER VERSES

Verses were only invented in 1560.

Today they mask the letters. Verses have attained an almost godlike status.

Because we have not known *The Story*, verses have become the measuring stick for what is "biblical." We have been flying blind without a cohesive story of the history of Century One.

We have had no model, no North Star to guide us through a starless night from generation to generation. Rather, we meander through a sea of fragmented sentences. We have no Global Positioning System, but only the guesswork of map-less men who discover new crumbs from verses which become temporary fads which temporarily give hope to starving Christians.

Question?

Which takes precedence . . . a group of verses which have been neatly joined together, or the sweeping, unbroken story?

Verses consist of a sentence or sentences that have tiny numbers attached to each one. If I take a verse here, and a verse there, I come up with some new, but shallow, conclusion. What if that conclusion contradicts *The Story*? Which prevails? *The Story* takes precedence over a verse. *The Story* ascends above any verse or a tapestry of verses.

The Story gives all of us a gyroscope, a North Star. Use of verses has taken us into every conceivable meandering directionless course. Random ramblings hardly equate with the divine inspiration of the Word of God. Place Paul's letters in their proper order, and that story will insist on emerging. All our versification of the New Testament must give way to *The Story*.

Come with me on the unprecedented journey back to Christian literature.

We have finished this book. Where does this leave us?

It leaves us in great trouble!

We are especially in trouble if we are among those who are committed to the Word of God. After all, we have now seen Century One. In so doing, we noticed there is virtually no resemblance between Century One and Century Twenty-One. In fact, how could we even call what we do in Century Twenty-One scriptural?

We have seen how churches were raised up in the first century. Everything about how we "do" church has no common ground with Century One.

Then we saw how Paul raised up workers. Our seminary way and the way Paul raised up workers bear no similarity.

As we lay this book aside, we each face a decision. Shall we continue being "New Testament" by our use of *verses*, in order to create that which is scriptural, or shall we use what actually happened back in the beginnings of our faith? *Verses* do not, and cannot, be used to show us what was *biblical* in Century One. Verses have no place in the greater panoramic scene of original practices. Either vast changes must come, or we must cease claiming that we are "New Testament." The choice is clear, but our faithfulness and our courage will be challenged. For those who have that daring, we must say, "Let your tribe increase," or "Let your tribe *begin*."

One of the first people who encountered this book made a rather simple, but telling statement: "The Christianity we have today is not the Christianity which God intended."

Let the revolution begin.

Books Which Show What The ChristianFaith Was Like "First-Century Style"

by Gene Edwards

Revolution, the Story of the Early Church

The Silas Diary

The Tutus Diary

The Timothy Diary

The Priscilla Diary

The Gaius Diary

The Story! Perhaps the best way we will ever understand what it was like from the day of Pentecost in 30 a.d. until the close of the first century is simply to know the story. Allow yourself to be treated to and enthralled by that story. (Warning: Knowing the story will change your life forever.) You will find that story in every detail, with nothing missing, in these *six* books.

THE CHRONICLES OF HEAVEN (EDWARDS)

Christ Before Creation

The Beginning

The escape

The Birth

The Triumph

The Return

Unleashing the Word of God

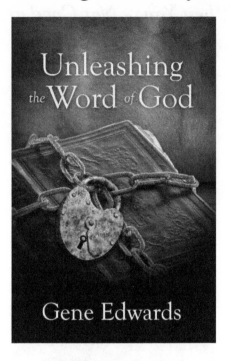

DVD Included

The DVD will shock you. It will prove without question why we cannot possibly understand the New Testament until we rearrange the epistles into their proper order. We presently work our way through the letters in a jumbled maze when we could read it on a straight super highway. You and I have never, do not, and cannot understand the New Testament. Think that statement is impossible? Wait until you see the DVD. We have not grasped the New Testament in its great panoramic scene because of the bizarre way the epistles are arranged.

Read *Unleashing the Work of God* and *Revolutionary Bible Study*. You will unleash the Scripture, and it will be a revolution. The chart you see in the DVD will show the sheer impossiblity of having a clear sight of the Scripture the way it is presently arranged.

Living Close to God
When You're Not Good at It

by Gene Edwards

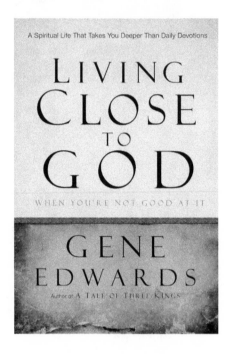

A Spiritual Life Unlike Anything
You Have Ever Read About!

There has been no book similar to this book in centuries. Here is a book for the "spiritually handicapped," the "spiritual failures," and the "spiritually incompetent." In other words, a book for almost all of us! A practical book on the "how" of a Christian's spiritual life.

In Chapter 1, Edwards places himself in the class of "the spiritually handicapped." You will revel in Edwards' failures at spirituality!

Expect to read unique, yet workable helps which have worked in the fire of down-to-earth daily living. It is spirituality for the age of static...computers, texting, cell phones, email...A triumph over the busiest, most demanding day.

THE AUTHOR

Soon after becoming a Christian, Edwards pulled apart his New Testament and rearranged its twenty-seven books in the order in which they were written. That was over four decades ago. As the final result, today he gives us a new and truly revolutionary way to study God's Word.

This book must be reckoned with, for it not only gives us a totally new way to understand the New Testament, but it liberates us from the old paths which have not served us well in understanding what God's Word is saying. Edwards is uniquely suited for this task.

While still eighteen, the author graduated from the university, finished his first year in the seminary, and was on his way to study in Europe. He later lived in the Holy Lands, and he retraced the complete journeys of Paul. He then visited all the major sites of the Reformation, then made his home in Rome, where he studied archaeology. (He was, and is, a student of both Latin and Greek.) After graduating from the seminary at age twenty-two, he became a pastor and then an evangelist.

Today he is part of the home church movement, and conducts seminars on the deeper Christian life. In all this, he has continued his pursuit of seeing the New Testatment as a forward-moving whole as over against stand-alone verses, and disjointed study of the Bible. Edwards is the author of thirty books, which have now been translated into eighteen languages for a total of seventy foreign titles. He is a frequent guest on national radio and television. He and his wife Helen make their home in Jacksonville, Florida.

CPSIA information can be obtained
at www.ICGtesting.com
Printed in the USA
FSHW010731101118
53665FS